VOLUME 16   SIL-TEL

THE PRACTICAL ENCYCLOPEDIA OF
Good Decorating
and Home Improvement

GREYSTONE PRESS

Alphabetically arranged and fully illustrated, your *Practical Encyclopedia of Good Decorating and Home Improvement* has been planned for your convenience and immediate use. In feature articles you will find a wealth of facts, ideas, suggestions, and advice that will help you solve your decorating problems. A Master/Guide at the back of each volume includes concise articles of historical interest, definitions of terms, and summaries of feature articles in the volume. Helpful cross-references appear throughout all volumes. On many pages you will find illustrations and descriptions of Project Plans and Home Plans, identified by the abbreviations PP and HP. For information on ordering these plans write to Good Decorating Plans Editor, Greystone Press, 225 Park Avenue South, New York, N.Y. 10003.

Appreciate and Care For Your Decorative Metal Vessels

Holloware, metal containers of depth and volume (as distinguished from flatware) for use at table and decoratively elsewhere, has been part of home decor for over 4,000 years. Admittedly, early collections usually were owned only by royalty and nobility; today a bride's first tabletop gift is often holloware. Candlesticks, trays, coasters, bowls, and sugarbowls and creamers are usually first gifts. Coffee and tea services, pitchers, and serving dishes (including chafing dishes) are glamorous additions to any home.

Holloware lends itself to creative use throughout the house (see below). Whether it be a family heirloom or a contemporary piece, holloware is considered a family treasure.

Metals used for holloware
Silver and pewter are by far the favorites. Silver has been a standard of elegance and beauty for millennia, and pewter, used by Oriental, European, and Early American designers, has likewise been in vogue for almost 2,000 years. Silver plate costs considerably less than sterling and is most often the first alternative; usually traditional, it coordinates with classic silver flatware. Gold electroplate has grown in popularity recently, is reasonably priced, elegant, and often

tarnish-free. Other materials to consider include copper, stainless steel, and combinations of metals.

Plating originated in 1742 when a silversmith in Sheffield, England, was repairing a copper knife and accidentally discovered that heat applied to silver caused it to adhere to copper. A major technical advance at that time,

Silver holloware belongs wherever your fancy chooses. A tea service flanked with candelabra on a side buffet table becomes, visually, part of every table setting on the dining table. Not reserved for company only, this silver still life gives daily enjoyment. Use of the sideboard candles as supplemental light can transform the ambience of the entire room, giving it an air of elegance.

Sheffield plate was abandoned in 1840 when electroplating, a superior method and more flexible for covering design areas, was developed.

Gold and silver plate today usually have a base of copper, used for its adaptability to intricate shapes when drawn or spun and its similarity to silver. Most applied borders, handles, and spouts are of cast soft alloys. Nickel plate is applied as the best fusing agent before the final coating of silver or gold is added by electrolysis. Quality plated holloware usually comes with a lifetime guarantee for the scientifically added precious silver or gold.

Pewter, a combination of metals, is the famous ware of many countries including the United States. In colonial times, this less-expensive alloy was used to make utilitarian pieces that have become classics today and can be used to complement both traditional and contemporary settings. Antique pewter contained lead, which caused its darker color and its tendency to stain, while modern counterparts are brighter, lighter, and less prone to tarnish or stain. Good quality modern pewter is composed of tin, antimony, and copper.

Points of quality

The price of holloware is determined largely by the size and weight of the piece, the amount of metal, intricacy of design, and apparent craftsmanship in its production. Simple raw or rolled edges and shapes are usually less expensive. Ap-

With holloware, just a little goes a long way; use it inventively. Classic silver candlesticks suit any evening setting, and can be used during the day if the candles are not lighted. Duplications in holloware gifts can cause delight instead of despair when used ingeniously. Matching footed compotes are ideal for a series of floral arrangements running the length of a table. Here, two are used to hold nosegay bouquets of baby's breath and rosebuds. Bonbon dishes take their turn as soup bowls at each place setting. Note that the cream pitcher is lined with gold.

Pewter is one of the subtlest ► tones in holloware. Its muted and darkened quality makes it particularly beautiful with subtle, elusive colors. Antique pieces used for line alone, rather than for serving, can be combined with modern easy-care pewter. Service plates can either be used atop china or, as here, by themselves. Most homemakers start with a few pieces of their chosen holloware pattern and add as the years go on. The beauty of pewter is ample reward for collecting.

plied cast borders are often found on better pieces, beautifully detailed.

When selecting holloware, check to see that the soldering is perfect at each seam. Pieces of best quality have one-piece borders with no break in decoration. Detailed outlines, as on some trays, are another mark of quality, as they require much additional hand trimming and finishing. Individual feet on footed pieces are generally most expensive.

Make sure that handles for hot servers are insulated and that interiors will not react actively with foods. Often silverplated coffee pots of highest quality are lined with 24-karat gold.

Choosing holloware

Choosing holloware that will best combine with other furnishings is both easy and exciting. Often holloware patterns are designed either to match or to coordinate with flatware. This gives a table a total look that is both elegant and traditional. In buying, it is a good idea to take along a place setting of your flatware and a small plate to see how well they coordinate with the holloware in question. Many holloware designs are so classic that they are universally compatible.

Small holloware gifts are always appreciated, but are especially appropriate for the traditional wedding anniversaries. Consider giving copper holloware for the seventh, stainless steel for the eleventh, silver for the twenty-fifth, and gold for the fiftieth.

Creative uses of holloware

Versatility is a major virtue with most holloware. It adds sparkle and brilliance to any room, and is especially effective when a little extra attention is given to proper lighting. A punch bowl can hold mail in the front hallway. Trays can give shape to a collection of small objets d'art on a living-room end table. Sauce boats can hold flowers and act as a charming centerpiece. Porringers double as candy dishes and candy dishes can hold relishes, nuts, or appetizers. Beautiful candlesticks belong anywhere in the home. These possibilities allow you to make frequent or steady use of your holloware rather than merely saving it for special occasions like weddings, anniversaries, or Christmas dinner. Aside from the extra cleaning that the increased use and display would entail, there is no reason why holloware should remain hidden away.

Care and repair

Follow the directions for cleaning and polishing provided by the manufacturer of your holloware. In general, food should not be left standing in any metal container. With normal use, little care is needed for either modern silver or pewter other than washing it with soap and water and immediate drying. For other than heavy stains or scratches on pewter, it can be restored with warm water and mild soap; rub gently, following the contour of the piece. Use silver polish occasionally on your silver to restore the lustre. Tarnish-preventive polishes make the regular display of silver holloware practical today. If the pieces are to be stored, however, they should be wrapped in a tarnish-preventive cloth and kept away from the air. Abused holloware can be returned to the maker either for replating or repolishing, but prevention minimizes this.

The minute scratches that form during the loving use of holloware are considered part of their charm and are called the patina. These, and the oxidized darkening that gives a decoration its depth and definition, should not be polished away. Enjoy them.

Give your holloware its day in the sun by using it outdoors. Any dining occasion is more elegant with the use of the hostess's best. A light summer repast that is as regal as an English high tea will be a welcome change from the casual cookout that graces most backyards. This table setting aptly illustrates that there is no limit to the amount of holloware that can be used on one table. The very quality of the reflective surfaces makes silver blend into the overall design of the setting, with the reflection of the garden in the polished surfaces. Minimal extra decoration is needed in this setting, which has as a focus a chimney full of small rose blooms, with chimney-covered candlesticks on either side.

Give Yourself Added Light And Ventilation at Low Cost

The practical function of a house is to furnish protection from the elements, but a dwelling becomes more than practical when it interacts with nature. An excellent way to achieve this union is to add a skylight, an ancient architectural device dating back at least to the Romans, who built the majestic Pantheon in the second century A.D. with an oculus at its summit—literally, an eye to the sky, admitting light and permitting a view of the sun by day and the moon and stars by night.

A contemporary skylight is likely to be made of glass or plastic and has the added quality of keeping out snow, rain, and dust while transforming an ordinary room into a special haven by drenching it in light.

Two views of the same skylight illustrate how it imparts a soft, diffused light to the planter area of a family room below, while on the top side it becomes the nucleus of a four-sided bench in the roof garden. Bubble-shaped acrylic of this kind requires no maintenance and is washed clean by rain and snow.

The addition of a long acrylic skylight over a modern ▶ dining room blends indoors and outdoors and permits a view of the tree canopy overhead. The extensive use of plastic in the ceiling window complements the glass, plastic, and metal of the interior, and the domed shape of the skylight lends height to a relatively narrow room.

Two fiber glass skylights, each 3 feet wide and 6 feet long, permit natural light by day. The one shown here, like its counterpart elsewhere in the room, is covered with a plastic panel to conceal fluorescent lights for nighttime illumination. The air pocket between dome and panel provides efficient insulation.

Skylights, in addition to creating dramatic effects, are frequently the most practical way of admitting light and air. In an interior room, such as a bathroom, or a room whose window opens on an air shaft, an overhead opening is particularly useful. Outside rooms that lack windows or that front on a public place such as a street where windows would entail a loss of privacy can be greatly improved by a skylight. However, even with windows, a skylight may be a desirable addition to a room that is unusually deep in proportion to its width and which has windows only on one end. If you do use a skylight in a room instead of windows, you will find it much easier to arrange your furniture since you will have more uninterrupted wall space.

Installation

If a skylight was not incorporated in the original plans for your house, you can still install one at modest cost. If you construct it yourself, the tools you will need should include rooftrees, foot planks, safety rope, hammer, handsaw, sheetrock knife, and, if applicable, a ripping chisel so you can safely remove the shingles and use them again. A nail puller and power saw will also be helpful.

Essentially, the installation involves cutting a hole in the roof, positioning the skylight, fastening it in place, and then rearranging the roofing material.

Some skylights are permanently closed. Others are equipped with automatic vents that open and close by means of a thermostatic control. Others can be opened manually, or with long poles, or by motor. The cost depends on the complexity of the mechanical apparatus involved plus the square footage of the window area. A double-domed skylight with a surface area of approximately 4 square feet can be purchased for less than $150. One twice this size would cost about $100 more.

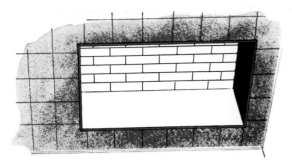

The simplest kind of skylight is merely a hole in the roof covered with translucent plastic. Housed in an aluminum frame, the window can be installed on a flat or pitched roof. Angle curbs to spread the light over a wider area are desirable, although these are not necessary if economy is of primary importance.

Manually operated skylights can be installed on asphalt- or slate-shingled pitched roofs as alternatives to more costly dormer windows. Consisting of two layers of glass on a wooden frame, these sandwich windows eliminate condensation and reduce heat loss. A drawback, depending on location, is that they may be hard to clean.

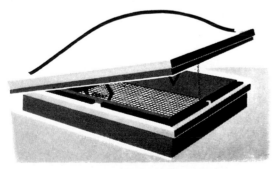

Free-blown acrylic domes can be incorporated into a house long after it has been constructed and can be used on any style of roof. Domes come in six standard sizes, either motor-driven or manually operated. Some include electric exhaust fans and movable louvers. The domes may be translucent or clear.

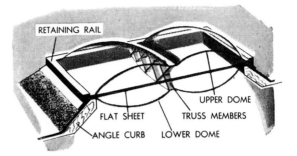

Two stationary domes with rigid structural support between them are recommended when illumination is more important than ventilation. The air pocket sandwiched between the upper and lower elements of the skylight provides excellent insulation. The angle curb allows the light to spread to all parts of the room below.

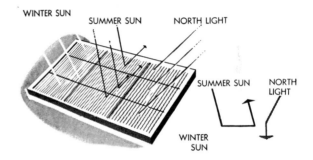

Tiny prisms inside this skylight deflect the strong direct rays of the summer sun and admit the more oblique winter sun and northern light, which are less intense. For maximum effectiveness, the skylight must be positioned on a north-south axis.

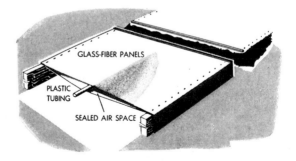

One of the most economical of skylights consists of two sheets of "laminated" fiber glass. A plastic rod between the layers creates the air pocket that acts as insulation. Installation is simple enough for most do-it-yourself carpenters. Translucent rather than clear, the fiber glass admits light while preserving privacy.

Discover the Practical Advantages of a Decorative Asset

Sliding glass doors allow the homeowner to enjoy the four seasons from the comfort of his easy chair. A spacious glass area lets the outdoors in during the day and provides the luxury of picture-window light.

When remodeling a room or a house, a sliding door can transform a porch or a sun room to a year-round room, making it more inviting. With a flick of a finger a movable glass door can be closed to guard the interior of a house against winter or, by opening it, let in the summer.

Contemporary sliding doors in general are well made, insulated, and can be easily installed by a professional or by the do-it-yourself enthusiast. Runner doors are available both in aluminum and wood in a wide choice of styles including French and Italian Provincial and Early American. They operate easily and require little or no maintenance after installation.

Sliding doors, in virtually every instance, add to the good looks and spaciousness of a room, making it appear larger than it is. Often the addition of sliding doors will enhance the value of a home.

Aluminum or wood

The choice between aluminum or wood frames is up to you; both types are good, if purchased from a quality manufacturer. Aluminum sliding doors offer a slimmer silhouette, durability, and virtually no maintenance. A wood frame that has been treated with a preservative against moisture, decay, and termites, and is properly painted or stained, will have a long life. Wood is also a natural insulating material.

Doors of both types should have insulating strips and be equipped with nylon or ball-bearing rollers. Many such doors will also be adjustable up to an additional inch in height.

Several types of hardware are available. In many cases the operating handle is separate from the locking handle and permits the installation of an additional lock cylinder by the homeowner.

Types of glass

The type of glass you choose for your sliding doors is of utmost importance. In some communities the building codes may specify that tempered safety glass be used since glass doors can be hazardous. According to a recent report by the now-disbanded National Commission on Product Safety, it was stated that, "Every year, about 150,000 victims of broken windows, doors, or glass walls discover that what they can't see can hurt them. About 100,000 walked through glass doors last year, probably believing the space to be open. If the doors had been safety glazed, most of the serious injuries would not have occurred. But the fragile, brittle panels of ordinary glass shatter even under a light blow from a child."

If you purchase a sliding glass door that does not have safety glass, it is strongly recommended that you decorate the door with decals or stick-

In this case, installation of sliding doors added to the spaciousness of the room. A porch that was located on the street side of the house was extended and enclosed. The result is an airy, comfortable room that is pleasant to be in at any time of the year.

Sliding doors installed in what was a screened porch turned this area into an inviting year-round room. The split-reed blinds over the doors and windows can be dropped when privacy is desired. Slate floor makes this inside-outside room easy to care for and the bamboo furniture contributes to an informal atmosphere. In winter, when the sliding doors are closed, sun shining through the glass adds warmth to such an all-season room.

Sliding glass doors let a flood of light into this comfortable ▶ family room. The use of glass: glass walls, glassed-in cathedral ceiling, glass doors opens up the room visually, creating a feeling of space, providing a fine opportunity to view the changing seasons, and effectively linking the outdoor and indoor living areas. For privacy, the multi-colored curtains can be drawn across the entire wall. This family room is an addition to a split-level house.

on strips to prevent someone from walking through it when it is closed.

The types of glass that come in sliding doors include plain glass, plain double-glazed glass, and triple-glazed glass. This last is used in extreme climates.

Prices for plain glass start at about 120 dollars for a two-section sliding door and increase up to 300 dollars and more for a triple-glazed installation. Screens usually come with sliding doors, as do storm panels if they are required. However, many of today's windows are set in a vinyl gasket that is permanent, leakproof, and maintenance-free. Such double-glass units require only screens.

Installation

Depending on the size of the unit to be installed, it is easier to set in a sliding door where a door or window already exists with a few feet of wall space beside it. If you are going to have the job done professionally, your lumberyard dealer is a good source of advice. He will also have brochures or several units installed on the premises, and can probably recommend a carpenter to do the installation.

Most sliding door units come in ready-to-install kits for the convenience of homeowners who want to do their own installations. The units come in both standard and custom sizes.

Generally a rough opening around the entire frame is required, about an inch larger than the sliding door. Headers should be 2x6s and vertical jambs at each end should be straight 2x4s. However, the correct size frame and materials to be used may vary depending on installation and location. Your lumber dealer can make up a list of the correct materials to use.

Complete Step-by-Step Instructions For Making Your Own

If you are a better-than-average seamstress, you can make your own slipcovers. They can be made to custom-fit your seating without your buying a pattern. And because slipcovers are not nearly as costly as reupholstering, they give you an opportunity to introduce bold and creative design into a room without making a more-or-less permanent committment to an adventurous decorating scheme.

Slipcovers can offer a cool, informal atmosphere in summer months, and can help disguise shabby or dingy furniture that no longer flatters the room's other furnishings. Slipcovers also serve to protect upholstery fabric through a few years of preschool wear and tear. And they serve well if you simply like a seasonal or more frequent change of pattern.

Preparing furniture for slipcovering is the first step, unless you are covering brand-new seating. If you are covering worn or faded upholstery, a little preliminary work is needed. Be sure the old upholstery is clean, and, if you have any doubts, call in a professional to do the cleaning job for you. It is well worth the investment in good, lasting furniture. Repair any sagging springs so that they are as close to each other as possible without touching, and are firmly sewed to the webbing or stapled to the slats. Mend rips and tears in the old covering. If some of the stuffing has flattened or hollowed out, fill in with new padding of good quality. Cover padded places with heavy muslin and sew to the original cover. The new slipcover will hide any patches.

Types of drapery fabrics suitable for slipcovers run the whole gamut of linen, chintz, velveteen, cotton, and cotton blends. Closely woven fabrics are necessary if the slipcover is to hold its shape. Since one of the advantages of slipcovers is that they can be removed and home-laundered, plan to select fabrics that can be washed rather than dry-cleaned.

In addition to the wide selection of drapery fabrics, sturdy cottons and cotton blends, including heavier wash-and-wear or permanent-press fabrics, are ideal for slipcovers. Corduroy, twill, and denim are also good choices. Also consider the possibility of stretch fabric for your slipcovers. Though such fabric may cost slightly more than others, its stretch properties will ensure a snug, neat fit to the finished slipcover. Some other fabrics that make up well in slipcovers include the lighter-weight fake fur or pile fabrics. Many of these can be washed and tumble-dried. Patterned sheets also can be made into slipcovers for bedroom chairs, although solid colors are the easiest to work with because there is no design to match. The majority of plain fabrics, however, will require contrasting colors in the piping or welting to give them additional interest.

As a general rule, patterned fabrics harmonize with either period or modern rooms, as do plain modern fabrics with interesting novelty weaves and textures. Allover flower patterns are always in good taste, but should be used on a small scale only in a small space, and on a large scale only in a large space. Checked ginghams and percales are smart and effective, especially for small chairs. For sun porches and family rooms, striped awning material and mattress ticking are both durable and striking.

To create a coordinated decorating scheme, slipcovers may be made of the same material

The slipcover's greatest talent is that of the quick-change artist. With only four slipcovers—and with a minimal outlay of the housewife's energy—the room shown here changes from winter to summer. In a couple of hours, the dark, richly patterned winter slipcovers can be replaced by pale, cool stripes. The slipcovers in this room also serve to integrate the decorating scheme by camouflaging the differing shapes of the unmatched sofas.

as the draperies. If the rest of the room has plain surfaces and solid colors, patterned draperies with matching chairs and sofas are unifying. If the rest of the room is patterned, stick with plain draperies and matching slipcovers.

Often the shape of the sofa or chair determines the choice of fabric; square or rectangular shapes accept stripes and plaids well, but curvilinear shapes should usually be covered in irregular patterns or with fabrics that have important motifs than can be centered on the back and seat.

Measuring for yardage

Measurements for slipcovers are difficult to take, and it is always wise to consult an experienced salesperson when you figure exact yardage. Yardage can be estimated in two ways: you can follow a fabric guide such as the one here, or, with greater precision, you can measure your chair or sofa.

Since the slipcover pieces must be cut along the grain of the material, the length of the chair sections is the controlling dimension in your calculations. Using a tape measure or a length of string, measure the length of the inside and outside arms, the depth of the seating deck and the front panel, and the depth of the cushion (top and bottom). Measure any strips needed to cover the tops of boxed back or arms and the sides of the cushion. Add 2 inches to all these measurements to provide a 1-inch seam allowance at each end. Also calculate the material needed for tuck-ins at back and sides:

3-5 inches at bottom of inside back, at back of seating deck, and at joint of arms and seating deck. If the back and the seating deck are to be covered with one piece, allow 6-10 inches for a tuck-in.

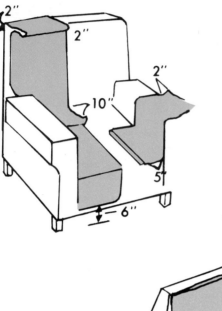

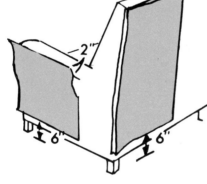

For a long sofa, take the measurement twice over the back and across the seat to discover any inconsistencies in proportions.

As a general reference for beginners, however, the table below will serve as a starting point. Take the overall dimension of your chair with you when you shop for fabric. The following yardage is figured for a 48-inch fabric without pattern or nap:

Arm or club chair	6½-7½ yards
Boudoir chair	4½-5 yards
Ottoman	2 yards
Cushion	1¼ yards
Love seat	8½-10½ yards
Sofa (6-7 feet)	10-14 yards

For 54-inch material, you can reduce this yardage by 10 percent. Additional material will be required in order to match stripes and plaids, for fabrics with nap or with a directional pattern, for flounces (see section below), and to cut bias tape for self-covered cording.

Necessary tools

Good equipment is essential to efficient sewing, and sensible preparation will make your work much easier. You will need, conveniently at hand, a box of sharp pins, tape measure, colored pencil or tailor's chalk, hand-sewing needles, heavy-duty thread, ironing board, iron, and sewing machine. Before you start to work, you should assemble any findings you will need: zippers or gripper tape, heavy snaps, and trimmings such as cotton cable cord, ready-made cord trim, or moss fringe.

Making a muslin pattern

The safest way for a beginner to make a slipcover is first to prepare a pattern out of muslin, fitting and cutting it on the piece of furniture. This method is actually cheaper and faster than working directly with your slipcover fabric. Mistakes made in the muslin pattern can be pieced and patched, which avoids wasting good material. Using muslin also saves on fabric yardage because you now have an accurate measurement. Having a pattern also allows you to save time and patience in matching stripes and prints. Moreover, you can make a new slipcover whenever you choose.

Fitting the muslin

The muslin should be pinned in place on the larger surfaces; corners and irregular portions can be patterned afterwards. If tuck-ins around the seat are required, ample material should be allowed for this purpose. The amount of materials you will need for a tuck-in depends on the degree of strain the chair's spring action places on seams at the back and side of the seat.

In pinning the muslin pieces on the sofa or chair, notch the seams with different groupings of notches three or four inches apart so that the pieces can be easily matched when you sew. These notches also facilitate matching stripes and patterned fabrics.

To determine the structural lines of your slipcover, follow the seams of the original upholstery. As you work with the fabric, you must watch the grain of the fabric to be sure that the piece is shaped correctly, that it hangs straight, and that no seams will be taken on the bias.

Measure the inside back from top to platform. Add 3-5 inches for the tuck-in. Measure the chair platform from the back of the seating deck across the front panel to 6 inches from the floor. Add 3-5 inches for the back tuck-in. The inside back piece and platform can be made in one piece with 6-10 inches added for tuck-in at back seat crevice. (These directions are for slipcovering a chair, since it is a small unit for a beginner to work with. However, you follow these same steps when fitting a sofa or other upholstered piece.)

Cut muslin according to measurements plus extra width on each side to provide a 5/8-inch seam allowance. Pin, starting from the center at the top of the chair. Smooth fabric down toward the seat of the chair. Shape around  the arm, clipping the seam allowance as necessary to fit curves. Allow at least a 3-inch tuck-in (A) and a 3-inch tuck-in at the back crevice on both the inside back and the seat (B). Fold back 3 inches for the tuck-in at seat sides (C).

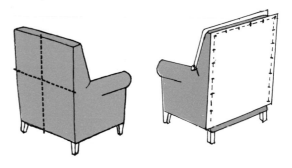

Measure the length and width of the outside back. Add 5/8-inch seam allowance and cut muslin. Pin the center of the muslin to the top of the chair at the center. Pin and shape down each side of chair to 6 inches from the floor.

Measure the length of the top band from seam where the arm and band are joined. Measure the  width of the band. Cut muslin strips. Start at the center top of the chair and pin muslin to the inside back and the back of chair. If necessary, shape with a seam at top corners of chair. Use 5/8-inch seams throughout.

Measure the inside edge of the arm from the outside roll of the arm to the platform of the chair. Add 3 inches at the seat for tuck-in.

Shape the muslin to the back of the arm to follow shape of the tuck-in on the inside back where arm joins. Unless there is a marked discrepancy in the size of the arms, only one arm need be fitted.

Measure the depth and width of the outside arm (A). Then cut the muslin and fit it to the edge of the inside arm and top band. Pin to the back muslin pieces.

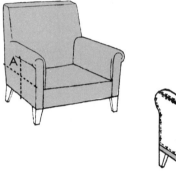

Measure length and width of the arm plate. Cut a length of muslin and pin and shape it to fit the arm plate. Pin to the inside and outside arm pieces. Allow 1-inch seams. The pattern for the arm plate

is pinned just to the platform on the inside front, but to the full length of the outer arm.

Measure the length and width of the top of the cushion. Using these measurements, plus the seam allowance, cut two squares of muslin. Measure the depth of the boxing and around half of the cushion's perimeter. Cut three bands to this length plus 4 inches. Add the seam allowance to the depth.

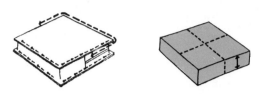

Mark all seam allowances in pencil before you unpin the muslin from the chair. Fold the back, inside back, and seat pieces in half to make sure they are even.

To determine the exact amount of slipcovering material needed, you must lay out the pattern pieces on the floor. Mark fabric width on the floor, lay muslin pieces within this width, then measure total length. Allow extra yardage for matching prints and stripes.

Cutting slipcover fabric

Remove seam-line pins from muslin pattern and lay pieces, right side up, on the right side of the slipcover fabric. Make sure that the length of sections is on lengthwise grain of fabric.

Center floral designs and match stripes on the lengthwise grain, and match plaids on both the lengthwise and crosswise grains. If you are using a print, center the major motif on inside back, on arms and outside arm pieces, and at front and top center of cushion. Try to match the inside arm pieces with the boldest part of the pattern close to the top of the arm.

Pin the pattern in place along the edges, then cut. Notch the seams.

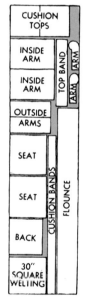

Even though you pin-fitted the muslin pattern, take the extra care to pin-fit the slipcover fabric. Muslin differs in texture and weight from other fabrics, so it is vital to careful tailoring that the fabric correspond to the chair measurements exactly. Follow the same sequence of steps you took when pin-fitting the muslin pattern, with the fabric right side out. Mark the seam lines with chalk (*not* pencil). Where seams require easing, make special marks at each end of ease line. Remove pins controlling ease, and place small gathering stitches or machine basting stitches between ease marks; adjust ease to fit adjoining section of slipcover.

Sewing the slipcover

Because the cushion is a fairly straightforward sewing job, it is a good place to start constructing your slipcovers so that you can accustom yourself to working with the fabric.

For a professional look, you may want to trim the slipcover with self welting or with cord covered in the slipcover fabric. To make your own cording, buy cotton cable cord in whatever size you want. It is available in a variety of sizes.

Cut strips of your slipcover fabric along the true bias. Strips must be wide enough to cover the cord and to leave a 1-inch seam allowance on each side. Sew bias strips together to make one long piece, joining them along the straight grain. Lay cotton cord in center of fabric strip, wrong side up. Fold fabric over and, using cording foot of machine, sew casing together. Stretch the bias strip as you sew.

allowance as you turn the corners. Stitch cording to slipcover ⅞ inch from cut edge, being sure that the cording stitch is concealed inside the seam.

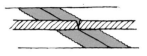

To join cording accurately, leave several inches of cord free at each end. Open cording seams slightly, and join the material along the straight grain. Cut the cords so that they just meet. Fold the bias over the cord and finish sewing trim to the cushion edge.

If you want to trim a solid-color slipcover with a contrasting cording, ready-made cord trim is available in solid colors. Apply it as you would custom-made cording.

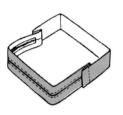

For cushion boxing, press two of the three bands in half on the length. Sew zipper between the two folded edges with a slot seam. Turn under 2 inches at the ends of the remaining band. Lap them over the end of the zippered band, and stitch, on the right side, 1½ inches in from the overlapping fold. Sew the upper and lower cushion pieces to the boxing; turn to right side through zipper opening.

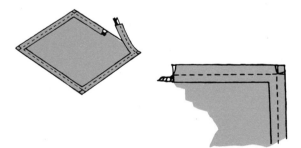

To sew finished cording to slipcover, lay it on the right side of slipcover fabric with the seam allowance of the cording along the raw edge of the cushion piece. Clip cording seam

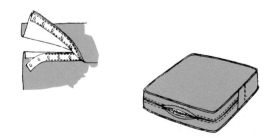

Gripper tape can be used as a closure instead of a zipper. Cut the two boxing bands 1½ inches wider than those used with a zipper; this allows a ¾-inch placket needed for the closure.

Next, make back section of chair. Sew cording around three sides of the back piece. Join the top band and sew cording around the front edge only. Sew outside back to the top band, leaving the seam allowance free at the lower band where it joins the arm. Sew the inside back piece to the top band, leaving the seam allowance free. Fit to the back of the chair.

Next, sew cording around the arm plate. Clip the cording seam allowance so it follows curve of arm. Join inside and outside arm piece. If you cord this seam, sew the cord to the right side of one piece first. Pin the pieces to be joined together and stitch. Then mark depth of the chair seat on the front arm plate. Sew arm plate to the arm sections from this point to the end of the outside arm piece. Fit to chair. Sew back section of outside arm to lower edge of top band. Sew around seam where the arm joins inside back piece, clipping seam allowance to fit curves. This seam (A-A) continues to the end of tuck-in.

Fit the seat of platform piece in the chair. At the corner of the seat, where arm meets front panel, the chair's spring action places some strain on the fabric. This point must be carefully constructed to take this stress.

Sew back and side edges to the inside back and inside arm pieces forming the tuck-in.

Fold the front piece down over the apron of the chair and pin the corner, forming a boxing. Clip the seam allowance at the base of this. Turn pinned corner to the inside of the fabric and seam. Turn to the right side. Sew the seam allowance below the clip mark to the arm plate.

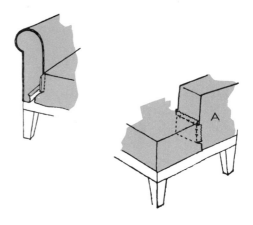

On a T-cushion, the spring action is at point (A). The seat should be cut with a 3-inch tuck-in at the sides but shaped to the front of the chair with just seam allowances added. The apron band is cut separately. At section (A), the boxing is made by inserting a square gusset sewn to the front armplate, inside the T, and to the seat side tuck-in.

Flounces

The flounce is usually 7-8 inches long, although the length may vary. Measure from the floor to the point where the flounce will be attached to the slipcover. Cut flounce the desired length plus $1\frac{1}{2}$ inches for hem and $\frac{5}{8}$ inch for the seam allowance.

Cut the flounce pieces across the fabric so that its long grain will hang vertically. Cut strips along the grain only if you intend to use horizontal stripes as a trim. The number of strips necessary will depend on the style of flounce you choose.

For a *straight flounce,* cut four strips the length of the chair sides plus seam allowances at either end. Sew cord or moss fringe to the bottom of the slipcover where it joins flounce.

For *inverted pleats,* measure depth of pleat at each corner. Add four times this amount to the distance around the chair. Cut strips to this length. Stitch seams underneath pleat.

For *box pleats,* pleat fabric strip to determine the size and depth of the pleats. Arrange pleats so they are evenly spaced with the center of a pleat in the center front. Multiply number of pleats by number of inches in each pleat. Cut necessary number of strips.

For a *gathered flounce,* cut fabric two to three times the distance around  the chair. Fabric weight and desired fullness determine the number of strips needed.

For a *circular flounce,* use heavy paper to make a circular pattern. As an example, measure two 16-inch lines at right angles. Draw an arc from one line to the other, forming a pie-shaped piece. Measure 8 inches up from the curve. Draw a second arc. Cut on this line for a circular flounce pattern. When measuring for a circular flounce, allow for a ⅝-inch seam allowance and a 1½-inch hem.

Cut a test piece of muslin from the pattern. Stay stitch along the seam line (the inside curve) and clip into the stitching. Stretch and measure the top. Divide the distance around the chair by this figure to get the number of circles needed to make a circular flounce. If the chair should need, for example, five-and-a-half circles, cut six, then take a little deeper seam.

If your print has a repet- itive pattern, pleat the flounce so that the design is evenly spaced and the major motif centered, if possible, in each pleat. If the pattern is too large for this, the design should be centered at the front of the chair.

For extra body, especi- ally if your fabric is light- weight, flounces can be  made double rather than hemmed by hand. For the yardage, figure twice the flounce length plus seam allowances. For a lined flounce, cut lining material 2 inches shallower than the flounce. Sew the lower edge of the lining and flounce together. Place raw edges together and press the hem. Sew the lining and flounce together at the top.

Slipcover closure

Use either a zipper or gripper tape for the back opening. The closing can go on either side of the chair.

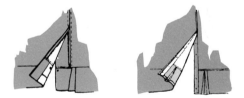

Sew one side of the zipper to the arm side of the back opening. Lap the corded edge of the back piece over the zipper and topstitch. This can usually be done close to the cording so that the stitching hardly shows.

The zipper can be sewed directly into the skirt on lightweight fabric. On heavier fabric, cut the skirt with an extension on the underside. Sew the zipper only as far as the skirt. Use a heavy snap to fasten skirt flat to extension.

Gripper tape is inserted the same way.

An exuberant floral print expresses the joie de vivre of summertime. A summer change of slipcovers offers a chance to experiment with unconventional and adventurous decorating that might seem frivolous in the winter.

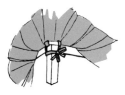

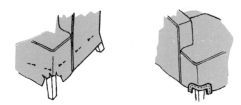

Sew tapes to the slip-cover at each corner over the leg. To keep the slipcover from riding up, tie tapes under the leg of the chair.

Make arm guards to protect areas that get the most wear and soil. Using your arm pattern, cut guards from slipcover fabric. Tuck in at the seat.

If you want your slipcover to fit like upholstery, leave off the flounce. Make slipcover to point of putting on the flounce. Put slipcover on chair. Chalk a line around bottom of chair apron. Trim slipcover 3 inches below line, and trim around chair leg, leaving a 5/8-inch seam allowance. Sew cording to this edge. Clip seam, turn to inside, and whip seam allowance back.

Cut a piece of heavy muslin to fit over (under) the bottom of the chair, inside the 3 inches of the slipcover flap. Sew separating zippers on four sides of muslin and along edges

Oyster-white linen slipcovers on the sofa and two chairs, a buff corduroy cover for the ottoman, and a dazzling collection of pillows establish a summery atmosphere that is at once bright and cool. Slipcovers are removed in winter to reveal the rich blue-and-green velvet upholstery. The abrupt switch in color and texture effects an unmistakable and satisfying seasonal change of character.

of the flap. Fit cover over chair, zip muslin on underside of chair. This holds slipcover firmly in place.

A sofa is slipcovered in the same fashion as a chair. If the back must be pieced, you may want to mark the divisions with cord trimming.

Some final cautions

As you may gather from the foregoing instructions, fitting and sewing a slipcover requires diligence. In the course of constructing a slipcover, you will constantly put it on and remove it to check the fit. Much of this drudgery can be avoided by making a muslin pattern. Nonetheless, you should stay stitch any edges likely to stretch as you work with the fabric, and be sure that basting is firm enough to withstand the stress of repeated fitting.

It is, ultimately, good fit that distinguishes the well-made slipcover. Although the task is within the competence of even a moderately experienced seamstress, you should remember to be patient with yourself the first time you do it. Subsequent slipcovers will give you greater and greater proficiency.

A seasonal metamorphosis of colors, shapes, and ambience occurs in the room pictured on this page. Slipcovers, of course, play a major role in the transformation from warm, mellow rusts, browns, and oranges to cool, soothing blues, greens, and whites. In addition, curtains, rugs, art, and accessories —even major pieces of furniture like the dining table—are rotated according to the season.

◀ Ready-made slipcovers like the well-tailored daybed cover shown opposite are generally available in department stores in a wide range of sizes.

SOFAS

Choosing Them and Using Them For Your Best Benefit

Sofa: the very word conjures up luxury, comfort, and inviting ease; sofa seating is cushioned, upholstered, supportive. Most likely the sofa has pillows on the seat and back, and padded arms, so the occupant is surrounded by soft surfaces. Sofa seating is used almost universally in modern living rooms from the most elegant French period rooms to rustic country retreats. The sofa's popularity as a furniture piece is well earned, for it offers just the right restful and relaxed seating for the informal life style so widespread today.

Choosing your sofa

Before considering style, fabric, color, or any of the myriad decisions of *taste* that must be made to choose the right sofa, it is wise to think ahead to the future. A sofa is a long-term purchase—one that is likely to see years of service —and it should be adaptable to future needs and altered settings. A sofa is a major purchase, too, because it represents a sizable financial investment. A carefully thought-out choice in the beginning means fewer decorating problems and fewer costly replacement purchases later. For instance, newlyweds starting housekeeping in a one-room apartment may foresightedly choose a love seat or studio bed for their first sofa. A few years later the same piece will serve handsomely for a guest room or library in larger quarters. Or families that move frequently— as do so many in this highly mobile age—may choose a pair of love seats or a sectional couch to obtain the greatest flexibility in room arrangements. The pieces can then be aligned, grouped, or even separated and used in different rooms as required.

Another general principle to keep in mind while shopping for a sofa is scale. Good decorating demands that the sofa be in scale with the space it occupies. A huge overstuffed piece, lavishly carved, tufted, and tasseled, may have been quite at home in a high-ceilinged old Victorian house with generously proportioned rooms, but it will surely overwhelm a small living room in a modern high-rise apartment complex. Conversely, a small, spare sofa will look lost in a large space. Large pieces belong in large spaces; smaller spaces require small-scale furnishings. With modern construction and upholstery techniques, scale is no longer tied to comfort. A sofa need *not* be large or heavy to provide comfort. The lightest and airiest modern designs may be just as comfortable as any of their more-plumply cushioned and upholstered predecessors; so relate the proportions of a sofa to the space it occupies.

In buying a sofa, it is not extravagant to choose the best you can afford. Quite the contrary—opting for the more expensive and better-built piece at the outset may prove in the long run to have been the most economical decision. The old adage, "penny wise, pound foolish," is particularly apt for sofa shoppers. A well-made sofa, constructed of durable materials, will give satisfactory service years after a cheaper piece has been discarded and replaced.

The muted elegance of the tan leather sofa in this comfortable family room can hold its own between the jewel-rich colors of Persian carpet and "Arabian Nights" wall hanging. The sofa teams well with the polished sheen of glass, chrome, marble, wood, and the black leather chairs; it is set off, too, by the all-white walls and floor.

Cost-cutting purchases

It may be, of course, that a more costly and better-built sofa is beyond your present budget allowance. If that is the case, there are cost-cutting alternatives that can make a choice sofa a reality without settling for a shoddy substitute. One possibility is to buy the sofa but delay upholstering it. The cost of fabric and labor for slipcovers represents a considerable saving over upholstering. Slipcover the sofa initially and have it upholstered later when your budget permits. Slipcovers have other advantages too. They can be removed for easy cleaning or replaced when a change of color scheme is desirable. Also, they can be tailored to tack onto the sofa frame, thus closely resembling the effect of real upholstery.

A second cost-cutting method is serial buying. Choose a sectional style and add additional pieces one by one as your budget permits. Be sure, of course, that the style you choose will still be available several years hence. Popular styles are retained by furniture manufacturers

Armless twin sofas, upholstered in an explosive Pucci print, offer a plethora of seating possibilities. They may be treated as one long unit; paired, face-to-face, across a coffee table; or separated at right angles to form a conversation corner. Sofas achieve a built-in, architectural look by matching their glossy yellow-lacquered bases to a platform end table. Other lacquered pieces also repeat colors used in the print for a coordinated look.

Quiet tone-on-tone room scheme derives richness and warmth from a variety of beautiful textures and materials; a deep-pile rug, highly polished wood, cut crystal, and bronze accessories, with a tufted contemporary sofa in a soft, taupe, crushed velvet.

over a period of years. Consult the store, and select a staple, classic, long-selling sectional.

A third way to cut costs is to choose a smaller piece—a love seat or a sofa bed that can be the nucleus of a second room in the future. The smaller piece—less expensive, but well-built and with years of service ahead—will be a fine start for a library, a study-guest room, or a playroom when the living-room sofa makes its long-awaited appearance.

How to recognize quality
To some extent, a sofa must be bought "blind." The fine materials and workmanship so necessary to a quality piece of furniture are hidden from view by the upholstery. A buyer often can-

not see for himself the webbing, the springs, or the frame, yet these important elements determine the quality and the cost of the sofa. Prospective purchasers must rely largely on the reputation of the manufacturer and the store. In some states, labeling of cushioning materials and spring sections is now required. Check to see if the sofa under consideration has such a label. One test for quality that buyers themselves can make is for rigidity. A sofa, which will be required to support several hundred pounds of weight, should have a strong, rigid frame. You can check the frame by lifting one end of the sofa. A well-made sofa will not sway or warp. While you are checking the rigidity of a sofa, look underneath. A well-built frame will have corner blocks in all four corners—not in the front alone—to brace the legs. If the bottom of the sofa has not been covered by muslin you will be able to see the corner blocks.

A well-built sofa generally will have the following features: tough, resilient webbing, firmly attached to the frame; coiled springs, set close together and tied with heavy, durable cord; layers of stuffing and padding over the coils; and finally the charming upholstery fabric that makes a finished sofa. Alternatively, it can be covered in muslin, ready to be slipcovered. The webbing may be of steel or textile, or wooden slats may be used instead. Coils should be tied to each other and to the frame as well. Poorly tied coils will soon break loose and play havoc

A fine example of exploiting two ideas simultaneously, this room takes chunky, massive, sculptured shapes of furniture and combines them with geometric painted racing stripes upon the walls and ceiling. The stripes are overscaled repeats of the sofa-fabric design, and the graduated widths of stripes give the room more depth.

with your comfort and with your furniture. Remember that a well-built sofa is never nailed. Good construction requires that joints be glued and doweled. Nails are a warning signal of cheap construction.

Modern sofa construction replaces the traditional spring-and-padding type of construction with foam rubber. Foam, which can be molded into any desired shape and thickness, is cemented to a base, and the upholstery is fitted directly over the foam. Furniture made in this way is far lighter in weight than traditionally upholstered pieces; it is mothproof and it is nonallergenic. Polyurethane is a less-dense material than foam rubber and offers somewhat less support, but it is also somewhat lower in price.

Sofa cushions may be made of feathers and down, a traditional and very satisfactory combination, with the single drawback that they mat down and need to be plumped up after each use. Foam or polyurethane cushions do not require even this minimal care. The least expensive, and least satisfactory, sofa cushions are those made with springs. With wear, the coils become sprung and the cushions turn lumpy, unattractive, and extremely uncomfortable.

Traditionally, sofa frames are made of high-quality hardwoods such as ash, birch, chestnut, or hard maple. In older styles, the frames were heavily carved, and ornately embellished and decorated. These older styles have much to recommend them in terms of beauty and craftsmanship but, on the debit side, they are dust-catchers, and hard to maintain.

Styles

Sofa styles are varied enough to fit every period and style of decor; there are pieces designed in the style of Louis XIV, French Provincial, Early American, Victorian, Chinese, and many more. With the advent of machine-age techniques and materials, sofas with frames of plastic, steel, and other man-made materials have been designed. Many of these newcomers to the decorating scene are both handsome and extremely durable. Sofas with external frames have also gained wide acceptance in recent years. The exposed frame reduces the abrasion

Diverse architectural elements demand strong unifying treatment. Here, color is used to bind together walls, library alcove, and elevated dining area, and goes on to a nonstop sweep of furnishings as well. Tangy orange spotlights the canted walls, is repeated in the vinyl floor tile,

velvet-upholstered sofa, and lacquered cube table. Deep blue walls, ceiling, and area rug emphasize the color value of the orange. Rounded sofa shapes are a softening note in the otherwise all-geometric room. Sofas are modules that can be rearranged in different seating plans.

and wear on upholstery fabrics and is therefore a practical as well as a good-looking approach to sofa design. In many cases the exposed skeletal frame is of wood. Wood endures as a favored material because the incomparable beauty of fine wood is still cherished and admired; the wood may be either solid or veneer. Veneers are sometimes mistakenly thought to be mere cosmetic cover-ups for inferior woods underneath, but this is far from being the case. Veneers are thin sheets of rare and beautiful woods. Glued onto well-made pieces of furniture, they make possible finely matched wood grains and greatly enhance the surface beauty of a furniture piece. It is an old technique, still used and valued today. (Beware, though, of poorly matched veneers or those glued by inferior furniture makers.) Sofas with fully upholstered legs, as well as seats and backs, are another modern design innovation. The overall upholstered look creates an unbroken line that is in a distinctively twentieth-century mood.

The two sofa styles particularly popular with home decorators today are the Tuxedo and the Lawson. Tuxedo sofas have arms and back of the same height. In the Lawson style, the arms are lower than the back. Lawson styling is at home in many periods, combining equally well with contemporary or older styles. When it is upholstered with a skirt, a Lawson takes on a "period" look; when the legs are exposed, it appears sleekly contemporary. Both Lawson and Tuxedo sofas may be upholstered in a tufted and buttoned manner for a traditional air.

Period-piece sofas, either treasured family heirlooms or charming, unique pieces picked up at auctions or antique shops, may keynote a delightful room setting. Remember, however, that if an older piece needs a complete rebuilding and reupholstering by a professional, the cost will be equal to that of a new sofa. The auction or antique shop "buy" is not necessarily a bargain.

Fabrics

The choice of a sofa fabric is closely tied to the mood and style of the room interior, and ranges widely from formal brocades, brocatelles, and damasks, through prints, plaids, and checks in wools, linens, and velvets to a kaleidoscopic choice of blends. However, there are several general rules that are worth remembering. If the sofa is used in a small room, relate the upholstery color to the colors of the walls, carpeting, and other upholstered pieces. The harmonious overall effect will visually push back the enclosing walls. If the room space is large, use

A window, framed picture-fashion by molding and hung with pinch-pleated curtains and tie-back draperies, serves as the backdrop for comfortably paired twin sofas that face each other across an oval coffee table.

Windows, walls, and floor of this room coalesce in a shell ▶ of neutral tones, a bland and unobtrusive counterpoint to vibrant red, orange, and green upholstery fabrics. Uninhibited colors, amply cooled by neutral background tones, are a surefire formula for redecorating tired rooms.

bright upholstery colors that contrast with the floor and wall colors. A bold, bright pattern used on chairs as well as sofa helps unify a large room that might otherwise seem spotty. Remember, too, that smooth, flat-surfaced materials such as satins, brocades, or damasks will show wear more quickly than will fabrics with a high pile such as velvet, velveteen, corduroy, and plush. Another important point: tightly woven fabrics wear better and longer than do loosely woven ones. Leather and vinyl upholstery, of course, are among the most durable and practical coverings of all. Other popular sofa-upholstery fabrics are prints in chintz, cretonne, and linen; smooth silks and satins; mohairs and other wools. Many new synthetic fibers, woven in a variety of textures and designs, are available too, with the added bonus of built-in stain- and spill-resistant finishes to make them practical and sturdy as well as decorative. Stain repellents can be added to all upholstery fabrics.

Lacy antimacassars are out of place and out of favor in most modern interiors but, nonetheless, they served a useful function in protecting upholstery at heavy-wear points from excessive soiling. The same result can be achieved today by having "sleeves" of matching upholstery fabric tailored to cover points of heavy wear. The sleeves keep sofas clean without intruding distracting fussy, out-of-character elements.

Sofa arrangements

Sofas should be arranged for easy conversational interchange. A pair of love seats or small sofas flanking a fireplace is an excellent arrangement. The strong focus of a room is usually a desirable location for a sofa and sometimes it is possible to create such a focus artificially by use of an accessory.

A sofa need not be centered along a long wall; place it close to a window and balance the rest of the room with another large-scale piece. Or arrange sectionals in a curve or U-shape around a coffee table. If the sofa does look best centered on the long wall, place side chairs to flank either end of the sofa and create an intimate seating center. In a large room, a freestanding sofa is a successful way to divide the space into more intimate areas. If the sofa does double duty as a bed at night, keep enough space free in front for the mattress to unfold or use a lightweight coffee table that can easily be moved. (See also *Dual-Purpose Couches,* Vol. 7, p. 1246.)

◀ Strong colors and a vivid pattern impose unity on the geometric shapes and surfaces in this arresting living room. The dominant red is tempered by a generous admixture of blue and white. Oversized proportions of the sofa are scale-matched by the upholstery pattern.

A romantic Récamier sofa is the focal point of a subtle blending of old and new. Cinnamon walls are a perfect foil for the pale wicker-and-chrome pull-up chair and flashing prisms of an exquisite tabletop crystal display.

What to Do to Lessen
Unpleasant Noise in Your Home

Sound conditioning, like air conditioning, is becoming a comfort feature that all families look for whether they live in houses or apartments. Living has become a lot more noisy as compared to thirty years ago, and constant loud sounds have an unfavorable effect on the physical welfare of all family members. Noise originates from many sources: TV sets, plumbing, heavy appliances, aircraft, vehicles, and people.

It is impractical and impossible to eliminate completely the many sources of noise, but it is practical and possible to control sound inside your house or apartment. Noise control should be considered in three main areas: ceiling, walls, and floor. In all three instances, noise control involves the lowering of *reflected* or *transmitted* sounds. For example, ceilings act as noise reflectors; sounds of conversation, appliances running, TV or stereo playing, and other sounds hit the ceiling and bounce back into the room. Walls and floors reflect also, but draperies and rugs cut back on this reflection of noise.

Ceilings

The most efficient way to reduce ceiling reflecting noise—by as much as 70 percent—is to install acoustical ceiling tile. Tiling materials and colors are available in a multitude of designs and hues that simplify decorating problems.

Installing acoustical tile is not difficult, and it should not take more than a weekend to do depending on the ceiling area. Details are explained in Vol. 4, page 718, under *Ceilings*.

Walls

Cutting down sound transmission through walls can be done in several ways. In existing homes the job is a little more difficult, but if you are planning to build (either from scratch or with an addition or remodeling) you should plan on sound control by yourself or with the builder. In existing homes, noisy sounds filter through walls because sound-deadening boards were not installed before dry-wall sections were applied. In such a case, leave the dry walls up and install sound-deadening boards on existing walls. This way, both cost and construction mess will be held to a minimum.

To do this job, first remove all trim. Electric switch and outlet plates should be removed, as well as duct grilles if you have forced-air heating. Sound-deadening boards, made of fiber glass and other materials, are available at building-supply centers; they come in 4x8-foot sections. They can be cut easily to fit small areas if the wall being covered requires fractional pieces. You can either nail or glue the sound-deadening boards to existing dry wall. If you nail, make sure you mark the outer board where the studs are located. Contact cement, however, is sufficient for adhering the boards, and the cement can be applied with an old 4-inch paintbrush or a trowel. Coat the existing wall and the back of the sound-deadening board and allow the cement to dry to a tacky touch. Apply the boards, butting the edges tightly to each other to ensure a snug fit.

Textured wall coverings can help reduce sound transmission through walls. Felt panels, framed by lacquered strips of wood, made this room more quiet during conversation or while playing stereo. Felt was affixed directly to the wall with contact cement. The material comes in various thicknesses and costs less than $3 a yard.

New dry-wall sections are applied over the boards by nailing. Tape and taping cement will completely eliminate all seams and nail holes, and the wall surface is ready for painting. Replace baseboard molding and electrical plates. It may be necessary to extend the electrical boxes to permit the plates to be flush with the wall.

The method just given is effective but by no means the most effective way to soundproof the walls in an existing house. Most effective would be to build a new row of 2x2 studs along each wall, spacing them ½ inch from the old wall, then applying the sound-deadening boards, then the finish wall—dry wall, paneling, or whatever.

If you are constructing a house, sound control between walls is much easier to build in. The builder should install a sound-deadening insulation—fiber glass, styrofoam, etc.—and then sound-deadening boards to the outside of the studs *before* installing the finished dry wall. The combination of insulation and sound-deadening boards practically doubles the efficiency of sound control between rooms. The cost for this added work should not be too high, but it is wise to get an estimate first.

If the builder wants too much money, install the extra insulation yourself. A stapling gun and a few hundred dollars worth of batten insulation are all it takes; having exposed studding makes the job quick and easy. If the house being built is two stories, install insulation in the joist space between the first and second floors; this will cut down greatly on noise between the two floors, and you will reap the benefits of lower fuel bills and more efficient air conditioning later.

Floors

Sound-controlling floors in existing homes is difficult except with adequate carpeting and underpadding. Thick-pile carpeting with under-padding cuts floor noise considerably. This may not be the least expensive approach, but it is the most effective in existing homes. If you own a one-story home and the basement ceiling is exposed, you can work between the floor joists to control sounds to the main floor.

Install insulation between the floor joists, using staples. Then nail sound-deadening boards to the floor joists, which locks in the insulation while providing an acoustical ceiling for the basement. If the laundry is in the basement or if the area is used for noisy activities by youngsters, all noise will be confined to the basement and will not reach the first floor.

If attaching sound-deadening boards to the joists is too hard a job, use acoustical ceiling tiles. Furring strips can be nailed easily to the exposed joists, and the tiles are light for easy positioning to take staples.

A quick and easy way to sound-control walls and floors in small informal rooms is to apply 12x12-inch carpet tiles. These tiles are about ¼ inch thick, and double-faced tape holds them securely in place. The variety of carpet-tile colors enables you to change color schemes easily, and they are easy to remove.

New construction permits you to build in adequate defense against sound transmission to begin with, and the same principles apply here: resilient materials and/or discontinuous construction. A resilient or spongy underlayment should be placed on the subfloor and then covered with another layer of protective ½-inch plywood before installing the final vinyl or hardwood finish flooring. This floating-floor type of construction helps keep down sound transmission, and here too carpeting and padding can notably lessen impact noise.

Control of noise at its source

Effective sound control must obviously take in not only the prevention of sound transmission but, more important, the reduction of sound at its source. Practically everything powered by an electric motor or connected to the plumbing system creates some noise. A kitchen or bathroom ventilating fan can be mounted in the

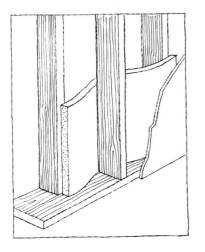

Staggered 1x3 studs nailed to a 1x6 plate is a proven technique that cuts sound transmission through walls. Additional sound control is done by lacing batten insulation through open space between stud and dry wall. Dry wall touches one stud only, diminishing vibration noises.

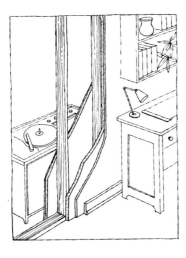

Sound-deadening boards nailed to studs *before* dry wall installation reduces noise through walls considerably. For added noise control, install batten insulation between studs before installing sound-deadening boards. Make sure board edges butt tightly together to eliminate all spaces.

Existing walls can be made soundproof by installing a new stud partition spaced about ½ to 1 inch from existing wall. Metal channel is set on floor near wall (1). Use 2x2 wood studs or, as here (2), 2½-inch metal studs. Sound-deadening board (3) is nailed to studs, then dry wall.

attic, connected to its exhaust grille by a fiber glass duct; result—less noise. Washer, dryer, dishwasher, refrigerator, etc., can be of the quiet type at slight extra original cost. Additionally, apply acoustical tile to ceiling and walls around them, and mount on resilient supportive pads.

Plumbing noises can startle and embarrass. Replacing the metal banding, hangers, and clips on pipelines with resilient substitutes will cut down on sound conduction. Insulate the collars of supports to reduce the noisy expansion and contraction of pipes, and wrap the pipes themselves in insulation, particularly when close to the house structure. The openings where pipes pass through walls should be tightly sealed with resilient material for proper cushioning. "Water hammer" knocks, as water is turned on and off, can be loud and startling. Air chambers installed at outlets can stop this.

Treat electrical installations to reduce passage of sound. Tightly calk all outlets. Never install outlets or wall switches back to back; they create noise funnels. Place outlets 36 inches apart on opposite sides of a wall. A switch and outlet should be at least 24 inches apart horizontally in order not to be within the same wall-stud space. To prevent the transmission of noise from room to room, place wall fixtures at least 24 inches apart on opposite sides of the wall.

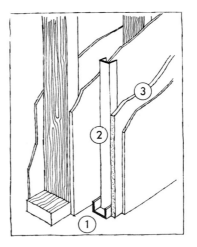

The Values You Can Find
In the Hispanic Idiom

Because of Spain's unique history, Spanish furniture styles of almost all periods differ from those of the rest of Europe. For more than seven hundred years—from the eighth century to the late fifteenth century—most of the Iberian peninsula was ruled by the Moors, Arab conquerors from North Africa. As a result, the styles and techniques of Islamic Moorish art had a pervasive and permanent influence on Spanish design. Even the famous Spanish tilework, so often used as a setting for Spanish styles, was introduced by the Moors, who brought the ceramic traditions of the Near East to Spain and Portugal.

Later, when Spain colonized most of Latin America, the same influences shaped the development of Spanish colonial furniture. Spanish and Spanish-colonial styles can therefore be classified together, and pieces of either type can be comfortably mixed in a decorative arrangement.

On the whole, Spanish furniture is massive and rather ornate. It combines the rich monumental quality of pre-and post-Moorish Spanish crafts with the finely worked decorative detail derived from Moorish art. Rich-toned walnut and chestnut are the most characteristic woods.

Accent or theme

Despite their formality and elaborate workmanship, Spanish pieces are surprisingly versatile. They can be used as dramatic accents in comparatively casual rooms without overwhelming them, and can easily serve as the focal point for an entire decorating scheme. In recent years they have become increasingly important as a major component of the relaxed but elegant "Mediterranean look" in interior design. Excellent and authentic copies of antique pieces can be found at moderate prices; many of them are made in Mexico. Modern adaptations that combine traditional beauty with contemporary functionalism are also widely available.

Distinctive touches

The Moorish influence on Spanish styles can be seen in several characteristics: the use of wrought metal in intricate arabesque patterns; the widespread use of leather, especially for chairs and often tooled or painted; ornately carved or painted finishes; and surfaces inlaid with detailed geometrical patterns of fine woods, ivory, and bone.

After the close of the Moorish period, the heavily ornate baroque style of other European countries had a strong influence on Spanish design. Sixteenth-century Spanish craftsmen began to carve furniture legs into massive spiral columns. *Vargueños* and *papeleras*—chests and writing boxes that were often inlaid and decorated with fine metalwork—became widely popular and are prized as the most distinctive creations of Spanish cabinetwork.

During the nineteenth and twentieth centuries modern European styles have exercised a degree of influence on Spanish design, but the older traditions are still very much alive and flourishing today.

Spanish furniture is associated with warm, even brilliant color schemes. Here, the massive spiral legs and fine wood of the table and chair, the carved doors, and the wrought-iron arabesque details of the sideboard are all characteristic features of Hispanic style.

The Pros and Cons
Of a Different House Style

As desirable building sites for homes have become more and more scarce, people have been looking with increasing interest at property that earlier generations of home builders and owners would have considered quite unsuitable. Sloping sites and hillsides that were previously ignored have now become not only acceptable, but, in some cases, even sought after. A result has been the creation of a house separated into levels to fit the contours of the land and a changed system of thinking about home planning and building. Such a house is the split-level, a multi-level house where each floor is staggered in relation to the next and the various levels are separated by less than a whole flight of stairs.

The split-level house was specifically planned for optimum use on sloping sites. A sloping site is not a requirement and the split-level can be used on flat plots, but a flat site frequently fails to do full justice to the fine external appearance that the split-level can achieve. Such use would be poor land planning, and only considerations of bad drainage, perennially wet soil, etc., requiring a shallower basement, are good grounds for locating a split-level house on a flat plot.

Benefits of separated levels

All the elements for compact, organized living can be built into a well-designed split-level home. The term "well-designed" is important here, for

implicit in split-level design is the concept of area zoning. Each zone of activity in the house is separated from the others vertically rather than horizontally, the logical consequence of a design that requires living to take place on different floor levels. There is greater and more efficient separation between sleeping, living, and "recreation-plus-utility" areas in a split-level

Here is an example of split-level planning that emphasizes horizontal lines rather than the pushed-together boxlike appearance that is so often associated with this style. The simple low-pitched roofs unite the two-story section of the house with the midlevel section and the garage. The aesthetically gracious exterior encompasses a 2,500-square-foot floor area that provides a convenience and comfort such as, often, only a split-level can offer. The entry hall eliminates having to walk through any room to get from one level to another. A door leading from garage into kitchen facilitates unloading of groceries, with enough space allowed between for a combined mud room and bath. Bathrooms on each of the three levels eliminate extra trips up and down stairs. On the lower level, a study and family room are exposed to daylight and fresh air since windows are above grade. Glassed-in sections of roof let in a flood of light on windowless side of house.

One of the great assets of split-level design is that it does not restrict you at all concerning the exterior appearance of your house. Look around and you will see split-levels in many different styles. If your taste runs to shingles and shutters, stucco with a red tile roof, or the natural look of wood against large expanses of glass, you will find that each of these is highly adaptable to this style.

If the exterior of your split-level is the type that requires painting, there is no limit to your color scheme except what your own good taste dictates. But do not be bound to any one color forever. There is no reason why, if your house has always been brown with white trim, it must remain that way. The next time you paint, change the color scheme and see how you have given your house a whole new look. You might change from brown to yellow with white and green trim, for example. Try green accents on the door and shutters, and your house will take on a handsomely updated look. To complete the transformation, add a low timbered fence to enclose the small entrance court, and a few carefully chosen evergreens for accent and to soften the appearance of the foundation.

The split-level plan of the house shown above is made evident on the exterior by the siding materials and by the architectural accents. The lower floor of the two-story wing is faced with brown brick, the upper floor by yellow clapboards. The demarcation of these two levels is further emphasized by the projection of the bedroom balcony. A deep overhang, which provides a 4-foot sheltered walkway from garage to front entrance, underscores the horizontal lines of the long single-story wing.

than is possible in a one-story house of comparable area. A two-story house has a similar separation, but the full-length stairway between the floors takes up a large amount of space that cannot be used in any other way. The location of stairs in a split-level plan tends to cut out most cross traffic and concentrate traffic flow into the best circulation patterns.

Less space is needed on a plot, leaving more of it available for a garden and the pleasures of outdoor living. There is also better provision for future expansion at the lower level.

Economic factors
If your budget or your property size is limited, a split-level plan can be a happy compromise

that gives you more house for the dollars spent on living space. A split-level needs less foundation, less roof area, less exterior wall than are demanded by a single-story house of corresponding area. The foundations need be only slightly deeper than necessary for crawl space alone. Utility area and garage can be left all or partly unfinished as they are located in the least expensive portion of the house.

Disadvantages of the split-level

As stated above, the split-level house is best in external appearance on a sloping site. On a flat plot, the house may have to be built to an ungainly height for accommodation of a lowest level partly above grade that includes the basic advantages of air and light. Additionally, a too-small split-level, perhaps lacking a carport or garage, has bad lines: too much height for its length, poor roof lines, awkward elevations.

There may be only illusory saving in the cost of building a split-level. It is harder to use mass-production methods in coupling the levels.

A variety of plans available

There are a number of approaches to planning a split-level home. They will vary with location, your budget, your family needs, and style of living. A frequent layout locates the living room, dining room, family room, and kitchen on the main level, with bedrooms on the upper level. A laundry and sewing center, game room, and guest room can occupy the lower level.

If you entertain often and on a large scale, another plan might be more suitable. Place entryway and living room on the main level; kitchen, dining area, and family room on the lower level; and bedrooms again on the upper level. Many variations are possible on these two plans and many other basic plans can be laid out.

The problem of building a home on a sloping site can be solved by erecting a split-level house. Careful planning and good design will produce a house that is both attractive and practical, and that appears to nestle into the slope as if nature intended it to be there. A split-level house can be built either with or without a basement. Without the basement, this type of house requires only minimal site preparation. The solution shown here is for an incline away from the street; such a plan is adaptable as well for lots that slope to one side.

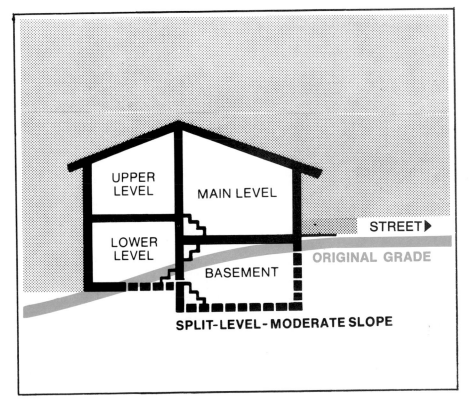

UPPER LEVEL

MAIN LEVEL

STREET▶

LOWER LEVEL

ORIGINAL GRADE

BASEMENT

SPLIT-LEVEL-MODERATE SLOPE

STAIRWAYS

A Primer on What They Are And How to Build Them

The stairway, an ancient architectural device for coordinating two levels, existed long before those discovered in the excavations of ancient Egyptian and Cretan ruins. One can imagine prehistoric man smoothing clay into steps on a steep slope or piling flat stones to make an entrance to his primitive home.

Building technology has improved greatly over the epochs, but the comfort and safety essentials of stair construction, based on human anatomy and movement, have long been standardized. If you are planning a new staircase, your architect may design one especially for your house. But many builders put together prefabricated wood or metal units, or compose a stair of stock parts.

The parts of a stairway

A stairway, basically, is composed of some seven major elements:

■ Tread: the horizontal plane of a step on which you actually walk.

■ Riser: the vertical area between two treads. Some contemporary open stairways (many of them spiral designs) omit the board that usually fills this area.

■ Stringer: the carriage that supports the treads and risers. There is usually one at each side of the steps. An enclosed or close-string stairway has two wall stringers; a conventional stairway has one open side and is called an open-string stairway.

■ Newel: the main post where the stairs begin and end and where landing junctions occur.

■ Baluster: one of the vertical posts connecting the treads and the handrail. Balusters plus hand-rail are called the *balustrade,* and both balusters and balustrade are often called *banisters.*

■ Handrail: the rail, usually of hardwood, that parallels the slope of the stringers from newel post to newel post. The rail may cap the starting-step newel, terminate with a decorative curve, or be crowned with a finial.

■ Landing: the platform between straight runs of steps in an L-shaped or U-shaped stairway. Also the top and bottom of a straight run.

A gracefully curved riserless stairway has a lightness to ▶ contribute to a colorful, texturally fascinating living room. To add solidity, the balustrades are uninterrupted rail-high wings finished in stucco. For comfort, safety, and good looks, the dark wood treads are carpeted. A curved staircase like this takes just slightly more space than circular stairs, facilitates carrying furniture upstairs.

A small backyard deck is a new addition in a formerly overgrown area. Steps to the outdoor porch consist merely of planks of redwood resting on a pair of notched stringers.

Cellar steps, originally walled in, were exposed when recreation area was built. Wrought-iron railings, a circle-end starting step, fresh paint, and a carpet runner all create a new appearance.

Unusually long for a straight-run stair-▶ case, this oak flight has a landing at the eighth step that is reflected in the pause in the ascent of the rail.

This L-shaped stair has a 90-degree turn at the landing. Steps and balusters are painted a creamy white and rails and newel posts are stained a dark tone for dramatic contrast. The foyer floor is an unusual composition of rough stones set in liquid fiber glass, continuing the theme of the Oriental garden.

An open and riserless stairway has supports accented in two colors to heighten the decorative quality. Wood plank treads are wrapped with a latex-backed carpet.

Safety requirements

A straight-run stairway that leads without landings from one floor to the next should not be longer than twelve or thirteen steps. If the flight will be longer, it is best to find space to introduce a landing. Turning steps, known as winders —wide at the outside and narrow at the inside —should be avoided. If winders must be used, install them at the lowest possible point so that a misstep will cause the shortest fall.

Ideally, a stairway should be wide enough to allow two persons to pass each other—a minimum of 3 feet. The conventional height for the rail is 30 inches on the rake and 34 inches on the landing; rails should be continuous, and

available on every step. Headroom should generally be from 7 feet 4 inches to 7 feet 7 inches.

The steepness of the stairway is a vital safety factor to consider. A rule of thumb states that the sum of the tread and the riser should be between 17 and 18 inches; a 7½-inch riser with a 10-inch tread, for example, is considered ideal for an interior stairway. Attic and cellar steps sometimes have to be steeper; outside stairways (short flights) can be shallower. A 5½-inch riser minimum and a 14-inch tread maximum are recommended outdoors.

Decorative aspects

The materials, finishes, and shapes of the stairway elements, from minute details to the overall sweep, contribute to the style of a stairway. Decoration also contributes to a stairway's visual impact and can be used to carry color schemes and style from one level to another. The basic tools you will use in decorating are color, pattern, and lighting. At the outset, certain choices should be made: for example, will the stairway walls match those of the upstairs or downstairs room, or be decorated as a separate unit? Will

A compact spiral stair in a remodeled town house not only saves space but makes a strong design point with its blocklike horizontal treads against vertical wall stripping. Stair leads to a balcony bed- and dressing room.

This dramatic staircase borrowed a corner from an over-large kitchen; space once filled by a walled, standard stairway was added to the living room. Note the superlative setting in which to hang the long, ornate chandelier.

Redwood, with its beauty and no-care qualities, is an ideal medium for outdoor projects. Here 2x4s, placed on edge, form the attractive wide, deep steps to a cantilevered "floating" deck, supported by posts and concrete piers at the outer edge. Upkeep is minimal; water runs off through the openings between boards. Ask for PP 3406-2.

the entire stair unit be painted one color? What sort of carpeting will be put on the stairway—choose for safety factors as well as color and texture. Accessories should also be considered. Finally, lighting should be carefully chosen for decorative possibilities and safety.

Earth packed against stringers and supports is a real enemy of wooden steps as is inadequate drainage. In time, moisture collects in soil and around support members, rots wood. Keep debris away from wooden supports.

To avoid injury to yourself or your family, or possible liability for injury to others, it is important that outdoor stairs be well constructed and in good repair. Check old steps for wear and damage, and paint them annually.

Rotten treads and stringers are quickly found by tipping steps away from house and probing into wood with a knife. If knife shoves easily into wood, steps are probably ready for replacement. Note rotted stringer (arrow).

Measure vertical rise from ground to landing, then divide by number of steps. To calculate step distances, tread and riser combined should normally measure between 17 and 18 inches. Stair should be at least 3 feet wide.

Two or more stringers are needed for exterior steps, depending on width. Place square on 2x12 stringer so 11-inch mark of blade, 7-inch mark of tongue lie exactly on edge, and mark. Bottom riser will be 1¼ inches shorter.

An alternate method of marking tread and riser cuts on the stringers is to use an old stringer as a template. Be sure to check measurements. Trace pattern lightly and use square to complete lines for accuracy and uniformity.

Mark 2x4-inch or 2x6-inch supports for stringers. These supports should be used even though stringers will be attached to porch or house. Supports and stringers are set on sunken concrete blocks or 4-inch concrete slab.

Join pieces by toenailing top of back leg to stringer and to the bottom support. For permanent placement of steps, nail tops of stringers to extended joists under porch. Other methods for placement of steps are shown in drawings.

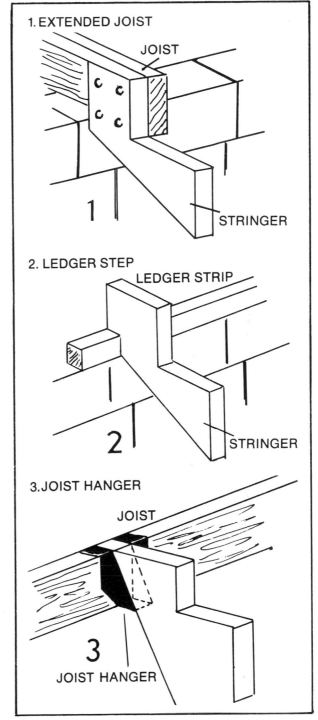

Here are three ways to fasten steps permanently: (1) If joists are parallel to stringers, extend joists and nail to them. (2) Notch stringers and nail to a ledger strip. (3) With joists and stringers at right angles, use metal hangers nailed both to stringer and joist.

Triangle of exterior-grade plywood or 1x12 stock is nailed to stringer and supports for extra strength. Nail to back along edges. Give stringers, supports, and reinforcing one or two coats of a brushable wood preservative for protection against dampness, mildew, and wood rot.

Nail risers to stringers after making sure the line between stringers is level. Buy the round-nosed treads from your building-materials dealer. If he does not stock them, buy 5/4-inch (1¼-inch) material of pine or fir for the treads. Round off front edge of treads with a plane.

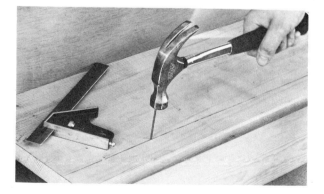

Now nail treads to stringers, making sure they are butted against risers. Allow about 1 to 1¼ inches of tread to extend beyond risers as nosing for treads. Use combination square as "depth gauge" to mark nailing points on tread over riser. Tack cove molding beneath nosing against riser.

If steps do not fasten permanently to porch or house, tip them over and nail risers to back of treads. This gives steps additional support and strength. For full precaution against rot, water damage, coat underside of treads and risers with wood preservative. Do this before final painting.

Fasten cove molding across top of top step and against porch or house. With nail set, countersink all nails and fill the holes with wood filler. To finish job, sand stock smooth and apply two coats of a good porch and deck enamel; allow ample drying time between the two coats.

Concrete Stairs

To prevent damage from frost, build 6-inch foundation that extends below frost line in your area. If soil is firm, inner forms are all that is needed—use double forms in sandy soil. When foundation is ready, cut out step forms—2-inch stock is best—and level on foundation wall as shown.

Nail riser forms to side forms, which should be perfectly vertical. Fill hole in foundation wall with gravel or cinders, then tamp fill thoroughly so it is well packed. Treads 10 or 11 inches wide and risers 7 inches high are standard dimensions for easy-to-climb stairs.

Determine tread size and cut side forms to fit riser. Be sure to allow about ⅛-inch pitch per tread—away from the risers—for adequate drainage and safety. If you bevel the front ends of the side forms, the risers will be beveled for added toe space. A 1-inch bevel is usually enough.

To support forms, place 2x4 supports edgewise against forms as shown. Nail forms to the vertical ties from inside. Wood stakes and 1x4 board hold lower end of ties in place. Tops of ties are held by 1x4s that are nailed at upper ends of each pair of ties. Leave room to operate float.

Pour concrete in bottom step and cover step with weighted boards. Pour remaining steps in same way. Puddle each step with float, before covering, to remove air. When concrete is stiff, level with float, finish edges with edging tool. Cover with moist straw or sacks for several days.

Ideas of Beauty and Practicality
That Anyone Can Use

Storage space, properly used, can make the difference between a serene household and a home where nerves are frayed, tempers are tried.

Ask a homemaker what she would look for first if she were shopping for a new home. Chances are she will say "the kitchen" or "the closets." And if she says the kitchen, she will probably list storage space as her primary requisite in judging its adequacy.

The frustrations stemming from poorly planned, inadequate storage space affect one deeply because they recur daily, and because at heart one knows they are unnecessary. Surely, you reason, you are not so possession-mad that no amount of drawers, shelves, and closets can possibly satisfy your needs.

In order to understand how to solve your storage problems, you must learn something about storage, its purposes, and uses before you can begin to take steps to apply the principles of efficient storage in your home. You must analyze your needs before you can apply the dozens of inventive storage units available. You must diagnose your particular storage handicaps before you can cure them.

Storage—an emotional subject

Ask a tired housewife at the end of a long day how many drawers she has opened, how many times she has bent and stretched and pulled items out of hiding places or looked for something that is lost and cannot be found.

Her response will be emotional. It is frustrating to feel that your possessions are controlling your time, your energy, and your ability to use them creatively.

Most people tend to react to problems of clutter and storage in one of two ways. One response is the neat-as-a-pin, everything-in-its-place approach. The other emotional response is to throw everything into a container and close the lid.

Flexible, attractive, efficient—this storage wall exemplifies all of the characteristics of a good storage piece. Combining open and closed units, it is an integral part of the room's decoration. Prints and art objects, strategically placed, lend variety to the bookshelves, and lighting is built into the unit.

Closed, these broad window seats seem to have just one bookshelf across their width. Open, the hinged top of each unit reveals an extra storage space in back of the bookshelf. This idea would be especially useful in a child's room for the storage of toys and games.

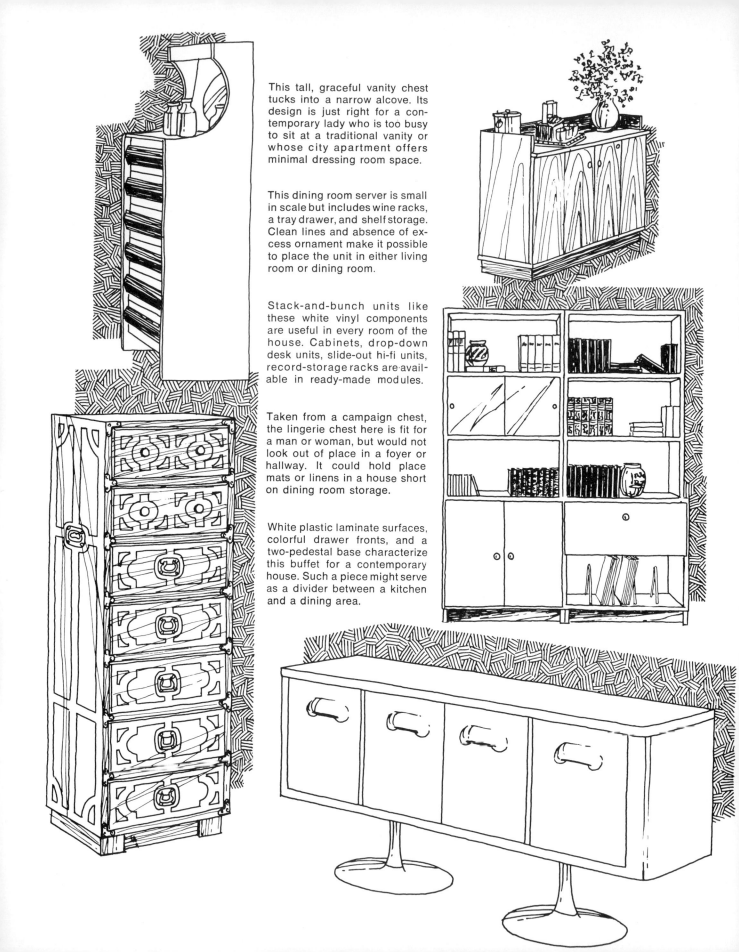

This tall, graceful vanity chest tucks into a narrow alcove. Its design is just right for a contemporary lady who is too busy to sit at a traditional vanity or whose city apartment offers minimal dressing room space.

This dining room server is small in scale but includes wine racks, a tray drawer, and shelf storage. Clean lines and absence of excess ornament make it possible to place the unit in either living room or dining room.

Stack-and-bunch units like these white vinyl components are useful in every room of the house. Cabinets, drop-down desk units, slide-out hi-fi units, record-storage racks are available in ready-made modules.

Taken from a campaign chest, the lingerie chest here is fit for a man or woman, but would not look out of place in a foyer or hallway. It could hold place mats or linens in a house short on dining room storage.

White plastic laminate surfaces, colorful drawer fronts, and a two-pedestal base characterize this buffet for a contemporary house. Such a piece might serve as a divider between a kitchen and a dining area.

It is important to know how you feel about the mechanics of storage before you begin to think about the practical problem of planning storage space. You can plan the most efficient storage in the world, but if you are the type who cannot be schooled to use the storage space properly, you are wasting time, money, and temper in pursuing a mad dream of efficiency.

This, of course, applies to the whole family as well as to the homemaker who makes the decisions about storage space. A beautifully planned closet may look wonderful in your back entry hall, but if your children are at an age when they think floors are for throwing coats on, you might be better advised to install a row of hooks for their wraps.

Individual needs

Storage is an individual problem for each family. You have a unique set of possessions and a unique pattern of life, so it is not possible to give you absolutes about the hundreds of ways to solve storage problems to fit your own specific needs. However, from the many examples illustrated here and the suggestions that are included in the text, you will be able to choose the methods and materials that will help to solve your storage problems.

Another vertical vanity has a hinged top with a mirror and a jewelry tray built right in. Its six drawers come in three sizes —shallow for gloves and scarves, medium for lingerie, deep for bulky items like handbags.

At the other extreme from cardboard boxes is a handsome veneered room divider. This elegant piece of furniture could be the focal point of a small apartment, and would also enhance a library or living room in a large house.

A sophisticated version of cardboard-box storage, sets of modular cubes provide infinite possibilities for storage. Suitable for any informal setting, they are available in fine woods as well as in colored plastics.

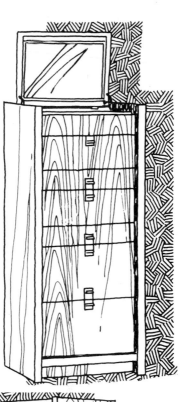

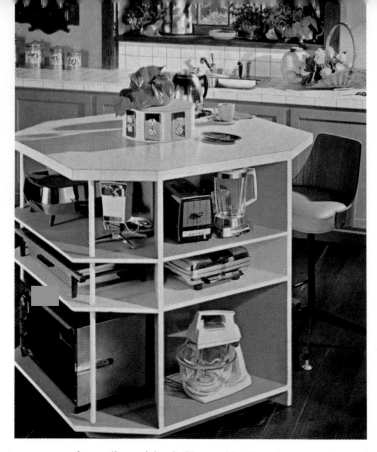

These solutions will depend to a certain extent on the kind of home you have. Modern houses with open plans and large areas of glass will not have as much wall space available as traditional houses; for modern houses, movable built-ins that act as dividing walls are one solution.

Individual taste must be served in planning the storage areas of your home. A kitchen is one room where this principle can be clearly demonstrated. Many women prefer a kitchen with open storage so that all the fascinating paraphernalia of cooking can be admired—whisks and sieves hung on pegboards, bowls and casseroles displayed on shelves, wooden spoons standing in a tall vase, spices ranged in racks near the stove, staples stored in a row of clear glass canisters. Other homemakers prefer closed cabinets and bare counters—everything smooth, slick, and wipable. It should be re-

An appliance island, this combination storage center and work counter radiates from a core topped with a circle of electric outlets. The appliances are taken from the shelves, set on the counter, and plugged in as needed. The shelves have been carefully spaced to accommodate appliances of varying heights. One section has been left without shelves, leaving knee space for a snack bar.

A guest room is hidden in this picture. First clue: the capacious storage drawers built into the frame of the sofa bed, convenient for storing pillows and bedclothes. Second clue: the drawers and cabinet in the coffee table, where the guest's personal belongings can be stowed.

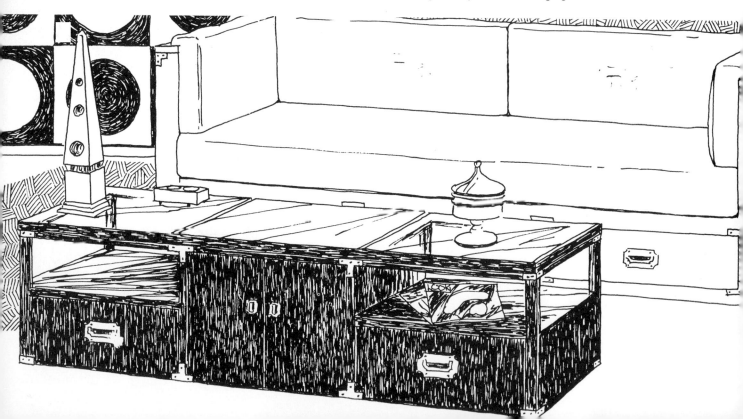

This bow-front cabinet, a handsome piece of furniture on its own, displays to full advantage a collection of antique clocks. Interior lighting fixtures dramatize the timepieces, which are set on glass shelves. The cabinet also protects these fragile articles from dust and breakage.

marked that the appearance of the open kitchen requires constant tidying to prevent disorder.

Flexible space

Besides satisfying your immediate and particular requirements, storage space must be flexible so that it can adapt to new purposes. The changing needs of a family through the years make this imperative.

The toddler needs open shelves, a toy box or bin, and large drawers he can reach easily to stimulate him to dress himself and care for his possessions. The growing child needs both open and closed storage; closed units to give him the

In an older house, you can put the walls to work to provide the extra storage today's homes need. Here, bookshelves and storage cabinets were installed in a living room. Backing them in a sun porch are tall storage cabinets that hold movie projector, games, phonograph records, and other recreation paraphernalia.

privacy he needs, open storage space so he can display his hobbies, collections, and treasures. He needs reachable storage space so that he is encouraged to develop habits of orderliness.

Adjustable shelves, trays, and vertical dividers, casters mounted on cabinet legs, pegboard—these are only a few of many available devices to ensure flexibility in the storage system you provide for your family.

You should keep an open mind when you shop for storage facilities. An eye for the ingenious can sometimes save you money. Rectangular wicker baskets, designed as letter trays, can be used to hold a child's socks or underwear, are light enough for him to carry from laundry room to bedroom without help, and will slide into open shelves to form "drawers."

Planning storage space

In order to ensure storage space that is adequate in both quantity and quality, you must start with a comprehensive plan that incorporates all the areas of your house. The efficiency of your bedroom closet can depend on the ade-

quacy of an out-of-season storage room in the attic. The efficiency of your refrigerator for food storage may depend on storage room in a freezer and on a good pantry. Your garage storage problem may be solved by building a little garden toolhouse in the backyard.

The sum of all the individual storage solutions adds up to an overall workable plan—and the overall workable plan helps you to think creatively about each of the solutions individually.

It is a temptation to believe that one more closet, another room, or a larger house will solve your storage problems. But the truth is that, for some people, more space simply means more clutter. Paraphrasing Parkinson's Law, clutter expands so as to fill the space available for its accumulation. Unless you are willing to analyze your storage needs and provide the kind of storage that will best meet those needs, you should settle for the clutter you now have.

The ideal way to plan the storage facilities for a house might be to start from scratch with an empty room or house, and then add only belongings for which you provide storage.

Most people, however, accumulate possessions in a haphazard way. You buy a small camera, for example, requiring only storage for itself and extra film; but this quickly leads to the acquisition of a projector and a screen and

The complex forms and brilliant colors of a traditional fabric provide an exciting and unexpected foil to the spare, precise lines of a modern storage wall for a dining room. The exposed dovetail joints of the narrow teak drawers are every bit as carefully and lovingly executed as the carving on the antique table and chairs.

slide boxes, and may eventually lead to the acquisition of developing tanks and an enlarger. The storage facilities for all this gear are likely to be haphazard also. Careful planning of your household storage will enable you to deal with the consequences of such random accumulation.

Basic questions

When you begin to develop a storage plan for your home, you must first find out:

1. What is to be stored.
2. Where it is to be used.
3. The best way to store it.

Besides these three basic steps, it is wise to anticipate future storage, within reason. If you have a toddler, you can predict that you will add a pedal car, tricycle, and two-wheeler to the carriage and stroller you now own. If you love to read, you can project a need for more bookshelves than you now require.

So, to your storage plan, you will add:

Step 4. What expansion room will you need?

An inventory of your possessions is one point of departure for a storage plan. You must know

This divider unit, finished to match the living room paneling, expands the comfort of both living and dining areas. The side pictured holds books, magazines, and hi-fi speaker. Accessible from the dining room are hi-fi turntable, buffet counter, storage for linens and serving pieces.

Overlapping shelves create a staggered series of pleasingly informal storage spaces—here a narrow shelf for small books, there a tall niche for display. This family room storage wall is finished with louvered cabinet doors made from stock-size shutters direct from the lumberyard.

what to store. The inventory should include detailed information about any furniture that provides storage space: a coffee table with a couple of drawers, or an unused dresser in the attic.

Another way to start is to list your family's activities, accounting for both work and play. By combining these two lists—equipment and regular activities—you will get a good idea of the needs your storage plan will have to satisfy.

For instance, have you ever counted the things that are stored in a fairly small area, the bathroom? If you tabulate, even roughly, the shampoos, cosmetics, extra tissue, pills, Band-Aids, the emergency first-aid booklet, the combs and brushes, electric shaver, massager, the hair dryer, the supply of extra towels, washcloths, sponges, nail brushes, and so on and so on, it will be apparent that bathroom storage consisting of a 12x12-inch medicine cabinet is inadequate and must be supplemented.

Or take a good look at the groceries in your pantry. There are many items that are always there, staples that are purchased every week or month: spices, sugar, coffee, and so on. The pantry will also house staple canned goods like soups and tuna fish, as well as emergency foods. The quantity of supplies you keep in stock is clearly limited by the total length of shelving.

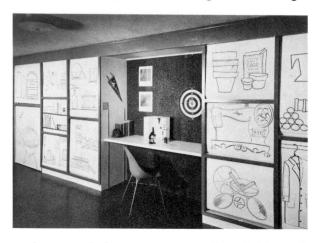

As you tabulate your storage list, divide each category into subdivisions that indicate frequency of use. For example, as you inventory objects used for serving and cooking, you should distinguish between items used daily, like dishes, cooking spoons, and saucepans, and items used only two or three times a week, like an electric skillet or heavy casserole. And finally there are items used only a few times a year, like a 30-cup coffeemaker, a chafing dish, or a paella pan. Each of these three categories presents special storage problems.

Locating storage space
In addition to listing the items you have to be stored and the nature and frequency of their use, you should analyze in what part of the

Between kitchen and dining room, this divider wall unit masks work areas. Space above allows air to circulate. When doors are closed, the unit has a serene, uncluttered look, partly because touch latches are used to eliminate visible hardware. Drawers hold silverware and linens.

Ingenious and fun, these open-shelf units are masked with ordinary window shades, installed at the top of each opening. The edges of the shades are concealed with 1x2-inch trim strips. These shades have been decorated with a felt-tipped pen, the drawings indicating the contents of each storage unit.

Open door of built-in tall cabinet reveals the artful design of the storage unit. Pull-out trays for glassware eliminate reaching and groping into the depths of the cabinet. Larger items, such as candelabra and serving dishes, are stored on the higher shelves.

house the items are most often used, so that you can determine the most convenient, accessible location for the storage you plan.

Sometimes this must be a compromise, and so you may have to list the place of most frequent use. Do you fill your coffee percolator at the sink before you set it on the range? Perhaps it should be stored at the sink, along with the tin of coffee and a measuring spoon.

In some families, an electric percolator might well be located in a bedside cabinet, where it can be filled with water and coffee the night before and set to start percolating five minutes before the alarm goes off. Again, individual preferences will dictate your location.

As an example of the detailed questions you will want to ask yourself in analyzing your storage needs this way, where do you keep your hair dryer? Do you stay in the bedroom, at your dressing table, polishing your nails as your hair dries? Or do you use it in the bathroom? Perhaps you wear the portable dryer at your kitchen desk, catching up on bills and correspondence or menu planning while your hair dries.

Each of these locations is a valid individual response to a situation, but each of the different answers would require a different location for the dryer, curlers, and you.

In deciding where things should be stored, look indoors and out for answers. Examine existing closets and storage areas that can be subdivided and made more efficient with racks, shelves, hooks, and dividers. Consider walls, staircases, and even ceilings. In the garage, you can lift large items to the ceiling with a pulley arrangement to provide winter storage for bulky gardening equipment. Or you can suspend racks from a basement wall or ceiling that will hold lengths of board or plywood until they are needed.

Go back over your inventory. Can furniture be moved to a new location to provide needed storage space? In almost every area of the house, you can find nooks and crannies waiting for you to put them to use.

Oak-paneled bifold doors conceal a family room bar furnished with running water and an alcohol-proof tile counter. The base cabinets contain bottles and extra glasses, thus relieving the kitchen of at least one storage problem. The bar, occupying a space only 2 feet deep and 6 feet wide, suggests a use for an unneeded closet or alcove.

Conventional storage methods

Almost any storage problem can be solved by using basic elements: shelves, bins, closets, racks, chests of drawers, filing cabinets, and other "holding systems." No matter what you decide to use, it is wise to test the solution before you invest in expensive equipment or furnishings that do not really solve your problem.

If you are not sure exactly what type of storage you need, test your storage ideas over a period of time. Use paper, cardboard, and fiberboard boxes and shelves, along with smaller boxes, plastic dishpans, even old shoe boxes or bags.

Arrange them and rearrange them, move them to different locations, test them in action. There are fiberboard bookshelves and sturdy steel

This custom-built storage wall is convincing evidence that storage need not be pedestrian. A dining room has been transformed by a series of cabinets that establish the room's architectural character. The shelves are designed to fit the various items they hold; here, shallow 6-inch shelves hold an extensive supply of glassware.

A number of shallow drawers is in many cases preferable to a few deep ones. These pull-out trays, designed for place-mat storage, discourage helter-skelter stacking and offer instant visibility of their contents. Top drawers contain silverware, which is also best stored in shallow trays.

shelves that come in many combinations of sizes and shelf arrangements at low cost. Use these in the activity centers of your house until you have made sure that the storage space is where you want it, in the amount you want, and that it really works.

After a time, you can replace the steel shelves or the cardboard bookcases with just the kind of furniture unit you want. Put the steel shelves to work again in the basement, attic, or garage.

This testing process is particularly important if you are planning to install built-in cabinets or wall storage in your home. Usually, built-ins are planned for fairly small rooms so that they will eliminate furniture and increase usable floor area.

Special techniques

If at all possible, include some information about the items in your inventory that will help you to determine the best method for storing them. Do you like tablecloths folded flat, or do you prefer them hung over rods? Do you have a large collection of paperbacks, so that bookshelves can be shallow and closely spaced, or do

A collector's cabinet holds Oriental art in its lighted interior and keeps the delicate figurines dust-free and safe from falls or scratches. The locked cabinet below provides storage for sculpture not on display.

you have a large collection of outsized art books that requires deep shelves spaced far apart?

Knowing sizes and measurements can speed the job of estimating how much shelf space you need, and sometimes just jotting down all this information starts wheels turning in your head. For example, knowing that only 6-inch shelves are necessary for most paperbacks may set you searching for hitherto-ignored space in hallways, along stairways, and on other "wasted" walls.

Identify with labels

It is often helpful to identify stored items. You can mark the shelves or cabinets, using a label printer and plastic tape, or using adhesive labels. Such identification is helpful if you store out-of-season equipment, like sleeping bags or blankets, on attic shelves.

Another reason for labeling is that every member of the family will know the location of everything, saving time and tempers. If you hire occasional temporary help—baby-sitters or cleaning women—they will be able to find things and replace them with a minimum of effort and questions.

On a pegboard, you can outline the various items you plan to hang, so that the silhouette remains to identify the proper location of a missing article. Just look at the outlined shape and you will know that that is the spot for the wire whisk in the kitchen or the wrench at the workbench.

For extra storage space, look under a stairway; otherwise-unused space can be put to good use. Game tables and folding chairs are stored in two adjoining cabinets, and there is even room for a third cabinet that holds a telephone and memo pad, with an extra shelf for directories.

Storage Furniture

There are many kinds of furniture pieces that can be used for storage, either alone or in combination.

Armoires

In a bedroom, an armoire can substitute for a clothes closet and do it in high style. Tall, bulky, and handsome, an armoire is a commanding piece of furniture. It can overpower the other furnishings in a small room, and must be chosen and positioned with attention to scale.

You can find sleek-lined, contemporary armoires that include lighted mirrors and a minimum of ornament. A beautiful antique ar-

A traditional bookcase provides both open and closed storage. It might be used alone, to occupy a wasted alcove; or it might be arranged with two or three identical units, to form a library wall.

This open bookshelf will fit almost anywhere because of its narrow width. You can use it to hold art books or decorative accessories. The shallow drawers separating the shelves are handy for storing stationery and pamphlets.

A rugged armoire might grace a dining room, a bedroom, or even a beautiful country kitchen. Its heavily distressed oak finish and elaborate wrought iron strap hinges invest this Spanish armoire with great force of character.

A man's wardrobe chest in pecky pecan grain has a solid, handsome look that would go well with many furniture styles. Shelves and drawers, both adjustable and stationary, hold everything in order.

moire may be used as a wardrobe in the bedroom, or, converted into a china cabinet or television housing, may confidently take its place in the living room.

Cabinets

Cabinets provide a most satisfactory method for storing a collection of small and diverse articles. The doors conceal the unavoidable clutter of such essentially untidy assortments as sewing and game equipment.

Cabinets also provide sensible storage for equipment and supplies that you want to keep dust-free. Behind its protective doors, the interior of each cabinet can be planned to organize stored objects in an orderly and accessible fashion.

Properly spaced shelves and vertical dividers are of paramount importance to a well-arranged cabinet. Linen cabinets, for instance, are often designed with widely spaced shelves, which are awkward, particularly if you rotate linens, since the high stacks widely spaced shelves necessitate must be removed whenever clean linens are added. A more practical solution is the use of shallow trays or adjustable shelves.

Although this low cabinet was inspired by a Japanese design dating back to the eighth century, its clean lines and antique brass mounts make it eminently suitable for a modern interior. Flush doors conceal shelf storage.

The grace of a French antique gives this storage piece its elegance. Cabinets like these might stand against stark white walls so that their curving design would be silhouetted.

This petite secretary—just 25 inches wide, yet providing bookshelves, drawers, and drop-front desk—demonstrates that you can find good storage pieces that are right in scale for today's smaller homes.

Chests of drawers

Though chests of drawers are most familiar in bedrooms as storage space for clothing, this by no means exhausts the number of purposes to which this versatile piece of furniture can be put. A low chest can be placed in a foyer to hold scarves, gloves, and extra car keys. A small chest next to a comfortable chair may serve as a sewing cabinet. In the bathroom, it might hold towels, soap, and curlers. In the kitchen, it furnishes drawer space for place mats, silverware, and tea towels.

Chests of drawers can be combined with bookshelves and cabinets to form handsome and practical, often inexpensive, storage walls.

Even after a chest has suffered years of wear and tear, it can be restored, refinished, repainted, and put to work again as blanket storage in an upstairs hallway or as general-duty storage in a playroom. A brightly painted dresser, each drawer assigned to one child, might stand at the back door ready to receive caps, mittens, and textbooks as the children return from school.

If dilapidation is irreversible, the drawers can still find a purpose in the attic as space for out-of-season clothing, or in the workshop as space for nails, screws, and small tools.

China cabinets

The traditional china cabinet has shelves protected by glass doors so that fine porcelain is not merely stored but exhibited as well. But the storage of china need not be so formal. A simple but effective china cabinet might be simply a strip of boxes hung over the kitchen counter,

This family room works—and works well, because it has been designed to provide storage for all the activities carried on in it. A built-in home office provides storage for typewriter and drafting equipment, and a built-in sewing center stores sewing machine and fabrics. Between these two work centers, a custom-designed storage wall combines open boxes and closed cabinets to accommodate reference books, game equipment, and decorating accessories. Drawers under sofa beds contain extra bedding.

◄ The heavy chest, a storage unit that probably predates all others, here acts as a living room catchall as well as a generously proportioned cocktail table. Its weighty form, heavy hinged top, and carved panels are impressively balanced by the massive Jacobean chairs flanking it.

In a first apartment, a steamer trunk found in a Salvation Army store becomes a combination towel rack and cosmetic cabinet. Its sides and drawers have been painted, its hardware polished, and its leather trim treated with saddle soap and elbow grease.

designed to hold dishes in an upright position, like so many phonograph records.

You can buy racks to stand on shelves to hold your dishes more compactly. Plates should be stored so that each stack is not too high; it is better to have two shallow shelves than one high one. Good china cups should not hang by their handles (with plastic cups, it does not matter).

In order to simplify your work and save steps, you might consider storing serving bowls and platters in the kitchen rather than in your dining-room china cabinet. You will be filling them with food in the kitchen. Platters and trays can be stored vertically in a narrow space.

File cabinets

Office-type file cabinets are invaluable for storing family records. They are, of course, available in standard steel office units. Enliven their appearance for home use by painting them in adventurous decorator colors. Some file cabinets are specially designed for residential use so that they simulate, for instance, colonial end tables.

A bevy of baskets is the unusual feature of this storage wall. The tags on the basket handles indicate the contents —everything from family papers to knitting wool—all anonymous behind their wicker areas.

Generous and well-planned shelf space offers efficient storage for file boxes, business machines, and stationery in a home office designed for serious work. Flush bifold doors also conceal the television when it is not in use.

Lacquered doors and walnut shelves are combined in this ▶ elaborate storage wall. Double doors hide a bar with a sink and shelves for glasses. The supports under the cabinets are plywood boxes sheathed in plastic laminate.

Use the file cabinets to store bills, income tax records, the children's school records, even recipes and magazine and newspaper clippings, appliance booklets, and garden catalogs. Buying an office file would strike an engaged couple as ludicrous, perhaps, but any homemaker of experience will know how useful such a file can be.

Whether the files are four-drawer or two-drawer, they can be placed in a row, with cabinets built in overhead for additional storage.

Hutches

Hutches, like armoires, hold a great quantity of equipment, but because they have open shelves

on their top halves, they do not loom quite so formidably. Hutches are traditional in dining rooms and kitchens. They display pewter or dishes on the shelves above, hold linen in drawers or enclosed shelves below.

However, smaller hutches have become popular for bedroom use, holding books above and clothing or linens below. You can even extend a built-in hutch along an entire wall, utilizing shelves for books and the base cabinets for storing important papers or photography equipment.

Hutches are especially suitable in kitchens that double as family rooms. Combining attractiveness with usefulness, they lend an air of cozy warmth to a room otherwise often uncomfortably functional.

Remember, however, that the top shelves of the hutch must be kept spotless and the contents arranged meticulously.

Magazine racks

Magazine storage space should be limited to inhibit the accumulation of back issues. You may, of course, purchase a specially designed wood or metal magazine rack to store current issues; this will prevent the unwanted buildup of reading matter on the coffee table. You might also construct a built-in magazine rack by mounting a tilted shelf on the wall and fixing a strip of molding to its lower edge to prevent the magazines' sliding off. The magazine covers will be easy to identify and will serve besides as a colorful and periodically changing decorating element.

If you keep a file of old magazines for reference purposes, they should be stacked flat on a shelf, their spines facing out so that the titles and dates of issue can be read. You may prefer to conceal the pile behind cabinet doors.

◄ These unusual modular units from Italy combine sleek steel and practical workability. Mounted on casters and built in compatible dimensions, they allow great flexibility of furniture arrangement. Here, the wardrobe placed at the foot of the bed and the stacking unit at the head provide a zone of privacy within a room.

Carefully planned storage turns a dining room into a multipurpose room. Closed cabinets in this demountable modular unit hold linen supplies and china. Center drop-down door reveals the makings of a home office: portable typewriter and adding machine. Below the desk unit are shelves that hold files and stationery.

Shelves

Shelves constitute a storage unit with almost universal utility. They hold foodstuffs, clothing, linens, china, books, tools—indeed, there is scarcely a room in the house that does not require at least some shelf space.

Bookshelves can be built under, over, and around windows and doors; in alcoves; or they can be tucked into corners. They can be free-standing or attached to the wall. You can buy suspension-pole bookshelves that can be dismantled in a few moments and moved to another location. And of course there is an almost infinite variety of sizes of unpainted units that can be lined up or stacked. You can place books on open shelves that form room dividers.

Regency-style hutch-buffet with bamboo trim is fitted with drawers, divided shelves, and pull-out trays. Here the elements store dining room accessories and linens, although they would be equally successful as a combination vanity table and chests in a bedroom.

This storage tour-de-force carries planned storage to a peak of perfection. The focal point of an apartment living room, it provides 27 feet of ceiling-high storage space to house everything from plant life through electronic equipment to a bed for the family dog.

Plan for the apartment storage wall opposite gives a clear idea of how much storage is built into the wall: (A) double-door storage, (B) display shelf, (C) adjustable bookshelves, (D) hinged painting concealing paperbacks and reference books, (E) dog's bed, (F) light-screen with retractable shade and plant display, (G) display, (H) television, (I) pull-out shelf with hi-fi, (J) record-album storage, (K) picture gallery, (L) game table, (M) storage behind hinged painting, (N) books and display, (O) drop-panel desk with cork facing, (P) two storage chests, (R) light-screen and plant display, (S) display, (T) walnut cabinet for trays and supplies.

And, of course, there are the traditional book-shelves designed as furniture, usually in finishes to match bedroom or living-room pieces. Book-shelves with glass doors or sliding panels offer greater protection against dust and casual wear and tear than do open shelves. A serious biblio-phile with an important collection of first edi-tions may insist on such protection. In the or-

dinary domestic interior, however, the closed look of these bookshelves diminishes to a cer-tain extent the decorating value of bright jackets lined up in easily accessible rows.

If you have a large library, you should esti-mate the numbers of books that will fit on con-ventional shelves, and those that will take larger shelves. The larger books should be displayed

on the bottom shelves, both for appearance's sake and because they are heavier.

Bookshelves can be tucked away into so many corners that it is possible to store books in many locations of the house, just where the books will be used. A set of shelves in the kitchen keeps cookbooks within easy reach, as a single shelf in the greenhouse stores gardening books for ready consultation. In the bedroom, a shelf on the headboard of your bed will be a convenience if you are a bedtime reader. Children's rooms should be generously provided with bookshelves to hold favorite storybooks, and a narrow shelf in the guest room may hold a varied collection of paperbacks.

A working counter conceals appliance storage in this kitchen island. The slide-out drawers that hold the appliances are rimmed so that nothing slides off. Shallow drawer under counter contains the cooking utensils needed to work with the appliances and adjacent range.

Storage space over these kitchen cabinets makes it possible to "file" platters and trays between vertical partitions. The open shelves keep everything visible and accessible. Shelving frame was built with a slight outward slope so that upper shelves are easy to reach.

Bookshelves can be installed in hallways and corridors, even on a very wide stair landing. A wide window seat with bookshelves framing the window is an appealing decorating treatment, and irresistible on a rainy day.

Shelves must be as sturdy as they need to be for the job they are doing; while a fragile glass shelf will be strong enough to hold cosmetic bottles in the bathroom, a carport shelf intended to hold heavy gardening equipment must be built of some more serviceable material such as redwood.

Lightweight prefabricated metal shelves mounted on the back of a door, or wooden shelves made of teak or maple, are suitable for storing spices in the kitchen. Shelves can be

Infrequently used party equipment, such as a large-capacity electric percolator and ice buckets, is best stored in closed, dust-free cabinets. This built-in buffet also provides shallow drawers so linens can be stored flat.

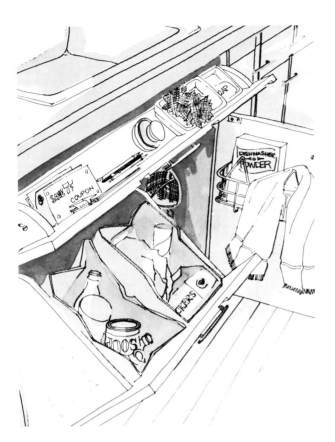

That little space under the sink can be wasted, or can be put to work like this. Swing-out storage unit holds soap, scouring pads, pot scrubber. Below, an outsized bin provides temporary storage for paper and trash.

Taking advantage of a tiny space left at the end of a counter after the dishwasher was installed, this shallow cabinet contains five shelves of canned goods stored one can deep. All labels are immediately legible.

made of rough boards supported by sturdy steel angle irons to hold basement items: paint cans, tools,· and out-of-season barbecue equipment. Shelves can hold a row of wine racks in a basement storage room.

For further ideas, see *Bookcases and Bookshelves,* Vol. 3, p. 546; and *Shelving,* Vol. 15, p. 2852.

Trunks

Trunks and chests furnish adaptable storage space, accommodating articles that can be folded or stacked or, even, as with toys, jumbled. Lovely mahogany sea chests with brass-bound corners and handles make wonderful end tables or coffee tables. They can hold playing cards and magazines or they can be equipped with bar fittings. If they hold lamps or other relatively immobile accessories, use them for storing financial records that you look at only once in a great while.

A curved-top trunk can hold blankets at the foot of a bed, a wicker trunk can hold toys or treasures in a child's room, and an old-fashioned steamer trunk can be used as a sewing chest.

There are fiberboard trunks that look like miniature Saratoga trunks. They are fun as well as useful; small enough in scale so that they can sit on shelves, they will store games, jewelry, or stationery.

You can add to the utility of a trunk by installing lift-out trays. Molding strips tacked

poses. Clean-lined tables with drawers can double as desks, especially if they are placed next to shelf-and-cabinet units. End tables can be little chests of drawers, or cabinets for storing articles you might be likely to use in the living room: coasters, cocktail napkins, playing cards, cigarettes. A coffee table can hold a complete bar.

In a room furnished with a sofa bed, end tables can be cabinets capacious enough to hold the bed linen and blankets the sofa bed requires. Alternatively, you can place the bed against a narrow, built-in cabinet topped by a hinged shelf that conceals storage space for bedding.

Fine silver is protected as well as dramatized by a tall cabinet that also provides drawers for the storage of silver flatware. The cabinet's formal design and antiqued finish correspond with the silver's classic lines.

horizontally around the interior walls of the trunk will hold the tray in place.

A large trunk, fitted with casters, might sit on your porch to hold baseball bats, gloves, tennis balls, and other sports equipment. When summer is over, simply wheel the trunk and its contents into the garage for winter storage.

Multipurpose furniture
When you are looking for freestanding storage, do not overlook multipurpose furniture that can be assembled and reassembled for different pur-

◄ This room divider provides storage space on two sides, acts as a dividing wall, yet avoids a closed-in feeling because the top and bottom are left open. Hardwood plywood, painted plywood panels, and inexpensive framing lumber are used. Send for Project Plan 3702-10.

Even when storage space is generously proportioned, it takes planning to utilize every bit of it. In this dining room closet, a tier of shallow, felt-lined silver drawers is tucked away in the bottom corner. In the center, glasses are stored on narrow shelves, while seldom-used serving pieces are kept on the top shelves.

The comparative virtues of folding closet doors are that, unlike sliding doors, they can open to expose the entire space and, unlike swinging doors, they require little area for operation. The handsome louvered folding doors shown here convert an alcove into a walk-in closet.

This modular unit is ingeniously designed to anticipate a growing boy's changing needs and interests. It provides shelves, drawers, rods, and hooks. On the inner side of one door, a clever shelf-and-string device holds tennis racquet, baseball bat, and rifles. On the other side, railed shelves contain paints and model-making gear.

Other Storage

In some ways the most effective solution to storage problems is the built-in unit. While the built-in can be a furniture piece, more frequently it is not. Whether it is a whole wall, a set of shelves, or a single unit fitted into an unused wall area, the built-in is an efficient and relatively inexpensive way to provide storage in the minimum space.

Built-ins

In some cases, built-in storage will function most efficiently if designed to house specific items—a television, stereo equipment, records, a sewing machine, or an ironing board, for example—then built to exact measurement. In other cases, you will want flexible built-in storage units. In a family room, for instance, you may not be able to predict exactly what your storage requirements will be, and thus may prefer to have large all-purpose cabinets.

Built-ins look best when they fit into the decor unobtrusively, as though they belonged as an

A closet needs accessibility and organization as well as size to make it truly practical. Here, folding doors give access to the entire closet. "Stacked" rods effectually double the closet's hanging space.

A well-lighted walk-in closet furnishes a comfortable dressing room as well as expansive storage space. This admirably ordered closet has high shelves for hats, low shelves for shoes, and a tier of narrow shelves for shirts.

A special closet for shirts and ties includes a mirror hung on the back of the door so that you can check the way your tie is tied. A set of drawers beneath the closet floor holds underwear and socks.

If you are searching for just the right shoes and bag to go with the dress you are wearing, it helps to have all your accessories lined up, clearly visible, and   good order. This ingeniously organized closet does just that, as well as providing a full-length looking glass.

integral part of the interior design rather than a tacked-on afterthought. Often this means matching wall color or paneling, or at least echoing the room's color scheme by painting the built-in with a harmonizing color.

Built-ins have some disadvantages: they cannot be moved and they limit furniture placement in the room. Also, they take up some floor space, though usually not as much as the furniture pieces they replace. In addition, semipermanent built-ins that are made to exact measurement and intended to house a specific item, such as a television set, are difficult to dismantle or convert to other uses.

The answer to the problems of built-in storage is often the use of storage modules, units that can be stacked and screwed together for a built-in look, then dismantled when you move or want to rearrange your furniture.

Whether you are assembling prefabricated units, giving directions to a carpenter, or making your own built-in, it is imperative that you design each unit of the built-in as carefully as you design its overall plan. In a storage wall that includes a hi-fi unit and speaker, a television set, or a desk, it is well to measure and remeasure units and to shift them to make sure that they are at the right height for greatest efficiency. If the hi-fi unit is positioned so that you do not have to bend or stretch, you will use it far more often than if you have to squat or stand on tiptoe.

Aesthetic values are not to be overlooked. Closed and open cabinets should be in visual balance. Display units should be placed for maximum visual impact, and the entire composition should present a general appearance of neatness and order.

In a man's closet, the racks for trousers and ties pull forward so their contents are completely visible. This careful organization illustrates how a great deal of storage can be built into a relatively small area. This unit could be built as a movable piece of furniture.

Step 1. After you have measured and marked the wall, carefully widen the closet-door opening, and extend the opening up to the ceiling. Remove the wallboard or plaster, and cut away the framing members. You can avoid laborious patching when the job is finished by working carefully to prevent damaging the plaster or wallboard at the sides of the opening.

Step 2. Install 2x4 framing in the closet. If the closet wall is load-bearing, reinforce the double 2x4-inch plate at the top of the opening with a 3x5-inch angle iron supported at both ends with a vertical 2x4 slipped between the wall surfaces. Nail the 2x4 to the wall stud behind it. This 2x4 goes in, whether or not you use the steel angle, to provide framing for the opening.

Step 3. From a single piece of plywood, cut the bottom of the overhead storage cabinet; notch it at both ends so that it will be flush with wall. Nail 1x2-inch cleats to wall studs to support cabinet at ends and back. Put in center divider of plywood. Nail door jambs to 2x4 uprights, and a strip on the double 2x4 wall plate, to make framework and wall surface flush. Hinge plywood doors to this strip. Fasten trim molding to door jambs and top plate. Build drawer unit of plywood, position it, and nail through bottom to the closet floor. Making sure that both sides are plumb, nail through bottom of storage cabinet into uprights. Drawers are simply plywood boxes with metal drawer slides. Install metal shelf brackets for adjustable shelves and put in hanging rods.

A supercloset that grows out of an ordinary-size closet is something you can create yourself, using the simple steps shown here. It includes several types of storage.

A medley of storage ideas

■ Look under and around furniture for storage possibilities. Tables that nest under other tables save space. Under the baby's dressing table you can roll boxes on casters to hold his toys or diaper supply.

■ Against a brick wall, you can build a Mondrian pattern of finished 2x4s, with crosspieces

A wall only slightly thicker than the normal partition provides convenient storage for folding chairs, card table, and snack trays. The flush door, extending the full height of the archway, is invisible when closed.

Most couples appreciate separate closets. In this well-designed pair of his-and-her closets, organization is ensured by built-in drawers intended to store socks and underwear, and overhead shelves to store infrequently used articles. Each closet is furnished with a mirror.

A wild zebra print inside this closet illustrates an important point about closed storage: since it is not always visible, you can be daring and imaginative in the way you decorate it. Bold colors and exciting prints can be used with perfect confidence in a clothes closet.

to form shelves. The waxed and gleaming wood and the texture of brick are compatible, and the shelves will hold small books and objects of art such as earthen pottery and stoneware. In the rectangles not used for storage, you can hang paintings or prints.

■ Borrow a planning device from ships' architects, who are notably ingenious in finding storage space in confined quarters, and install drawers under a boy's bunk bed.

■ Store vases in open shelves above the potting bench or in a special cabinet in the kitchen.

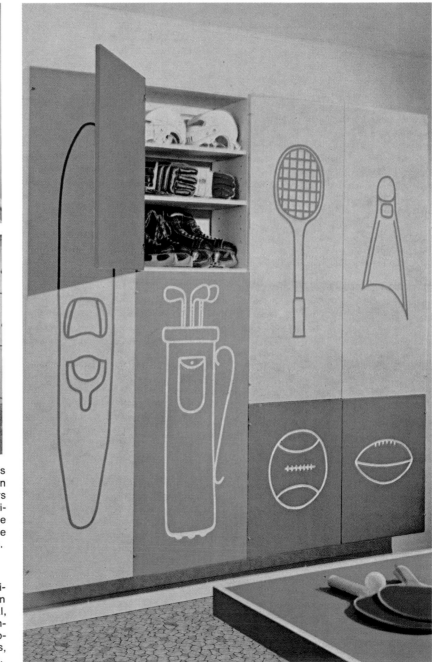

Equipment for a large bridge party is stored in the small closets shown in these two photographs. Folding chairs are enclosed in a 29-inch-wide cabinet at one end of a built-in storage unit. At the other end, a 14-inch-wide cabinet conceals folding card tables.

It is amusing to see outlines of various pieces of sports equipment on these storage cabinets—and practical, too, for the outlines signal what is inside. Lockers are sized to accommodate specific items: small for skates, larger for golf bag, largest for skis.

Keep them all in the same place so that you can find just the right container each time you arrange flowers. In a plastic dishpan on the same shelf, store the frogs and flower holders and florist's clay you will need. A cup hook on the bottom of the bottom shelf will hold your garden shears.

■ Kitchen storage should be grouped by the three major work areas: the sink, the range, and the mix-and-bake center. Try to make it possible to reach and lift each thing stored with one hand. By building shelves close together, you can fit more shelves into the available space and thus reduce the necessity of stacking bowls and saucepans. (See also *Kitchens,* Vol. 10, p. 1860; and especially Vol. 11, p. 1959 ff.)

■ Use very high shelves to store items that you will not use often. In winter, store the ice cream freezer on your highest shelf; in summer, store Christmas cookie equipment there.

■ You can partition drawers with wood divider strips to "file" kitchen tools. You can also buy partitioned plastic trays designed to store flatware, small tools, thread, and other sewing aids.

■ Before you fasten a rack on the inside of a door, make sure that the rack will clear the wall when the door is closed.

■ Sewing storage is unworkable unless it is partitioned, measured, planned. Use dowels to hold spools of thread, either on a rack or in a drawer. Try not to combine the sewing center with another activity (writing desk, for instance). If you must leave sewing unfinished, try to work out a screening arrangement—louvered doors, or cabinet doors that slide over the work center. (See also *Sewing Centers,* Vol. 15, p. 2842.)

Clothes closets should be at least 24 inches deep and should provide at least 3 feet of rod space for each person using the closet. Place rod from 5½ to 6 feet from the floor, depending on height of person who uses closet most. (See also *Closets,* Vol. 5, p. 818.)

■ One foot of bookshelving will accommodate eight to ten books. Along with regular bookshelves, why not include a tilted shelf for dictionary, encyclopedia, or magazine display?

■ Clothes hangers are 16 to 20 inches wide. Garment bags are 63 to 69 inches from top of hook to bottom of bag, and 23 inches wide. Allow enough room for both.

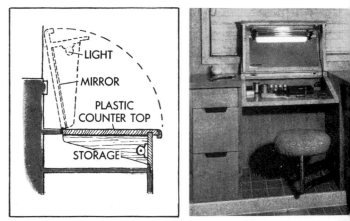

A useful extra in this bathroom is a vanity table that holds a large amount of cosmetics safely tucked away out of sight so that the bathroom stays neat. The countertop includes a lift-up lid that reveals a mirror, light, and storage room for makeup.

Because of their small size and often-cramped arrangements, bathrooms demand a knowlegeable use of minimal storage units—units that fit in tiny unused spots and provide a maximum of storage area. Two such units are shown on this page. The first, pictured above, measures a slim 36 inches in width, 10 inches in depth, and is hung directly on the wall. The unit provides ample space for storing toiletries and stacks of linens, and even for displaying knicknacks. The bottom section of the cabinet is a tilt-out compartment that holds soiled linens and clothing. The unit is a do-it-yourself project, PP 3402-1. The second storage unit, shown at right, employs the neglected space around the flush tank. Here, the storage area consists of a system of partitions and shelves where linen, toiletries can be stored, a towel rack, and a slim-jim cabinet where cleaning items can be kept. This is also a project for the home handyman.

How to Build a Built-in

Use a combination square to lay out the slots, then cut with a saber saw, or with a handsaw and chisel. Slide the top into place; nail to cleats across the back and to the uprights. Use finishing nails and glue for fastening.

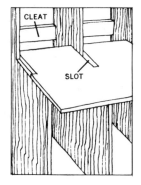

You are now ready to add the facing and molding as shown in the illustration below. Whenever possible, use facing strips of dimension lumber in standard widths so that you need not do any ripping. For this project, you cut lengths of 1x2 pine for the upright pieces. Notch the end pieces with a handsaw to receive the cross-pieces. To ensure good fit, nail and glue the facing strips to the end upright strips after notching, then measure between them for the horizontal strips. Cut the horizontal strips, and nail and glue them to the vertical strips. Then measure for the remaining intermediate uprights. By following this system, you should get good tight joints be tween all facing pieces.

To finish the trimming, nail lengths of cove molding around the top of the unit at the ceiling line. This molding covers the ¾-inch gap you left to allow you to tilt the basic components into position. Miter the molding at the corners. You can come close enough by marking the 45-degree angle with a combination square and cutting it with a handsaw. If you like, cut and fit this molding, but do not nail it into place until you have painted the rest of the unit. Then paint the molding to match the ceiling, nail it on, and touch up the nailheads. This way you do not have the tedious task of painting the molding while trying not to smear the rest of the built-in. Nail a 1x3 board around the bottom of the unit, mitered at the corners, and then nail lengths of ½-inch quarter-round molding on the top edges. Also nail ¾-inch half-round molding around countertop.

To make the bookshelves, cut pieces of plywood or lengths of 1-inch pine. Cover the raw edge of the plywood with wood edging tape (you just apply it with contact cement), or cut the shelves a little narrow and then fasten ¾ x ¼-inch strips of pine to the edges with brads and glue.

By far the easiest way to hang the shelves is with adjustable metal shelf strips. These strips are screwed or nailed to the uprights, then little metal clips are inserted wherever necessary to support the shelves.

This step-by-step explanation of how to build the ceiling-high breakfront shown on these pages will give you an understanding of the way most built-ins are constructed. Even if you do not build this particular installation, a grasp of the construction principles involved may help you to design your own built-in storage.

Most built-ins are essentially made up of boxes. In the unit shown, there are three basic boxes. Start by building the two end boxes; these stand against the wall with space between for the center box. A bottom piece fits into the center section, and a countertop bridges all three sections. You then add facing and molding, hang the doors, and put in the adjustable shelves.

But one must begin at the beginning. Using a power saw, cut four L-shaped upright panels and three bottom sections of fir plywood. These form two boxes for the end sections. Now stand these two sections against the wall, having first removed the baseboard. When you remove the baseboard, you will either be able to see the stud locations or tell by the placement of nails on the baseboard where the studs are. Use your level to project the stud locations up the wall to the 1x4-inch crosspieces. The upright panels are made ¾ inch less than ceiling height, so they will tip into place easily. Position the boxes so the space between them is equal to the width of the boxes themselves. Check with a level to make sure the sides of the uprights are plumb. Then drive screws through the 1x4 crosspieces into the wall studs.

Fasten another bottom piece between the two upright units by nailing short cleats to the two end sections, then fastening the bottom piece to the cleats. Also nail in a cleat across the back between the two units at the height of the countertop. This need not be fastened to the wall and

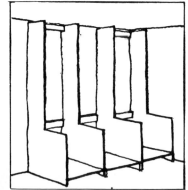

can be set out from the wall for ease of nailing. It will support the back of the countertop.

Cut the countertop with notches and slots to fit around the uprights as shown in the illustration. The easiest way to locate the lines along which to cut is to lay the plywood top in its place on the completed part of the unit and mark the places where it touches the uprights.

The flush doors in this unit are the easiest type to make since they are just rectangles of plywood with no special edge treatment, but they are probably the hardest to hang because they have to fit exactly. Start by carefully measuring the door openings. Cut two doors for each opening that are about 1/16 inch larger all around than the measurements call for. Hold a door panel in place with the hinge side tight against the facing. If the door opening is not exactly square, you can easily

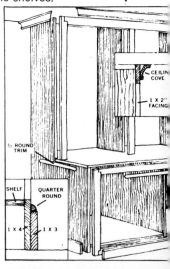

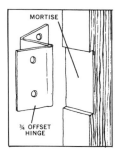

MORTISE

¾ OFFSET HINGE

tell how much you have to plane off the top or bottom of the door to make it fit properly.

When you have planed the door to fit the opening with a little less than 1/16 inch clearance, top and bottom, cut mortises for the hinges with a wood chisel, screw on the hinges, and hang the door. You can use ordinary butt hinges for flush doors, but ¾-inch offset hinges give more support.

Now fit and hang the second door of the pair as you did the first. The doors should overlap slightly when you try to close them. Close one door over the other and mark the overlap with a pencil. Remove the door you have marked and plane away half the excess. Also, bevel the inside edge back about 10 degrees for clearance, as shown in drawing. Rehang the door and use it to mark the remaining excess on another door. Remove this door and plane away the edge to your mark. Rehang and try the two doors together. They will probably still be a little tight, so carefully plane the edges of each, without taking them down again, until you have a uniform clearance of slightly less than 1/16 inch when closed.

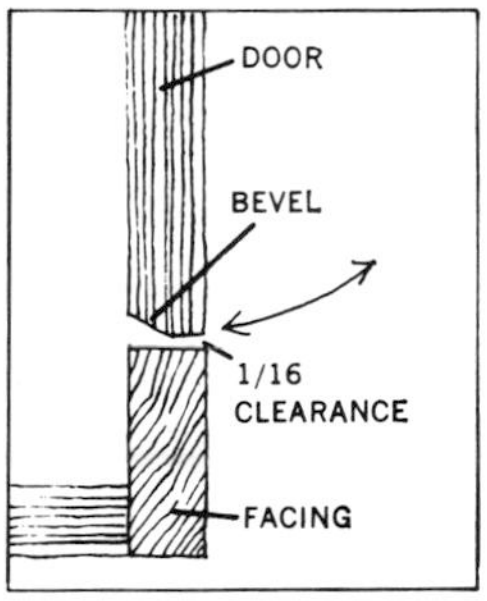

The lipped doors shown below are another type of door often used on built-ins. These are probably the easiest type to fit because you have ⅜-inch clearance under the lip to make up for any inaccuracies. However, you must cut a ⅜ x ⅜-inch

DOOR

BEVEL

1/16 CLEARANCE

FACING

rabbet on three sides, and this is difficult to do unless you have some type of bench saw. You can round over the outside edges with a router or plane, or just bevel them back about 10 degrees with your saw. No edge treatment is necessary if you use fir plywood and paint it.

You hang lipped doors with ⅜-inch offset hinges of the type shown in the drawing. Screw them on the doors first, then hang the first door, allowing for a little clearance all around. Now when you position the second door, you should find that it fits without any planing or complicated techniques. Leave slightly less than 1/16-inch clearance between the doors.

Overlap doors give a built-in clean, contemporary line, but they require careful fitting and edge treatment of the plywood. However, no facing is required on the built-in itself, and the semiconcealed pin hinges you use (either of the two types shown) let you set opposite-opening doors next to each other. Either of these two types of hinges, when installed, is practically invisible when the doors are closed, with only a

tiny part of the hinge pin showing. The hinges also have slotted mounting holes so you can adjust the door position slightly to compensate for errors. You still have to fit the doors carefully beforehand, however, because you do not have much room for error. Allow for any edge treatment when measuring for door sizes.

Drawers are not too difficult to build if you can use a table saw or a radial arm saw. There are many methods for making drawers, but the easiest and best way for most built-ins is shown in the drawing below.

You start by making a drawer box to fit the drawer opening, fastening on the type of drawer front you want later. This way you can fit in the box to work smoothly without having to worry about how the front fits. When the drawer works well, you just screw on the front to line up properly.

Before you make the drawer box, you must decide on the type of drawer slide you want to use. You can simply fasten wood strips to the inside of the drawer opening, then cut ¼-inch deep grooves in the drawer-box sides to ride on the strips, as shown in the drawing. In this case, the drawer box should be the width of the opening, less about 1/16-inch clearance on each side.

You can also use metal drawer slides, which do not require any groove in the drawer sides and work very smoothly. These metal channels, which are prefabricated, glide along complementary metal guides fastened to the inside of the cabinet. However, you must allow ½-inch clearance on each side of the drawer for the hardware. This will necessitate a lipped-front construction; drawer front must extend ½ inch on either side.

Use ½-inch plywood for the four sides of the drawer boxes, with ⅛-inch hardboard for bottoms. Cut a ⅛-inch groove ¼-inch deep in all four drawer sides, about ½ inch up from the bottom edges. The hardboard bottoms slip into these grooves as you nail the drawer box together. When the drawers are fitted in place, make flush, overlap, or lipped fronts for them. Clamp on each front, then screw through the front of the drawer box into the front.

OVERLAP DOORS

SEMICONCEALED PIN HINGES

CABINET DIVIDER

1 X 2" CLEAT

HINGES FOR ADJACENT DOORS

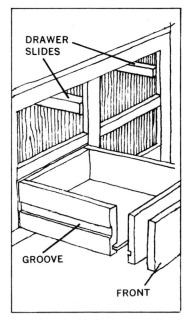

DRAWER SLIDES

GROOVE

FRONT

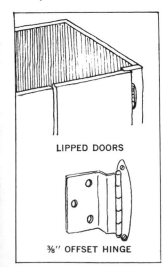

LIPPED DOORS

⅜" OFFSET HINGE

Almost everything you need for taking care of your backyard can be tucked away in this ingeniously designed storage shed. Garbage cans, mower, cart, and garden tools hang on pegboard, stand on shelves, or fit into racks. Doors hold shelves and a fold-down table. Construction is of plywood, perforated hardboard, and dimension lumber.

Back view shows how firewood, waste containers, and garden equipment are stored in a special niche. The wood deck of the shed should rest on concrete-block or pressure-treated wood piers, spaced 3 to 4 feet apart. To make sure the deck is level, set the first pier at the highest corner and use a level to set the others.

Diagram shows how the shed is put together. The 2x6 beams bolted to the sides extend out in front to support the roof overhang. Framing for the floor section is similar to the roof. Four 2x6 beams, 10 feet long, run the long dimension of the floor. Use 2x6 spacers to keep the joists rigid. Sections are fastened together with ⅜-inch bolts. The revolving rack that holds small hand tools is mounted on a dowel secured by pipe flange.

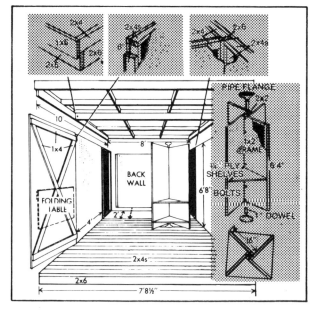

■ A man's suit, if trousers are folded over the hanger, requires 3 to 3½ feet from hanging rod to floor. If trousers are hung on pants hangers, they will need 4½ to 5½ feet. A woman's dress will require from 4 to 5½ feet, depending on her height and the length of the dress.

■ To label a little child's storage drawers and cabinets, use pictures instead of words. Designate the proper storage place for garments and toys by pasting a picture of the article on the front of the drawer. Then the child can help put away his belongings.

■ To make stock cabinets and shelves look built in, bolt them together for more solidity, change hardware, and paint with enamel for a smooth, luxurious look.

Serious gardening inevitably requires an enormous amount of equipment and supplies—power mower and clippers, bags of peat moss and fertilizer. Besides providing plenty of space for storage, this tidy potting shed offers a charming bonus in the form of a children's playhouse.

Storage for sports equipment is provided in this two-section box that also serves as a bench. Individually hinged tops minimize the strength needed to open the chest. Six 4x4-inch posts form the framework; the panels are 2x2s backed by decorative copper paper.

■ You need 12-inch-deep shelves for dinnerware, except for large items like platters and serving pieces. Shelves only 4 inches deep will allow you to store glasses in a single row, a safety measure that eliminates groping at the back of a shelf for glasses of the right size.

■ If you display dishes or trays on a shelf, be sure that there is a stop to hold the dish in place. A quarter-round molding strip will hold them.

■ Store table linen so that the stacks of linen are low. Flat trays that pull out are best for this.

■ If you have a one-story house, store cleaning things in a rolling cart that can be wheeled from room to room as you work.

■ Have two spice racks. Keep a small one near the range. Store larger supplies of spices in a cool dark place, where they will better retain their flavor.

■ Try not to use your kitchen counters as storage space. You should have room to prepare meals without constantly shifting little items. Appliances may be installed on pullout racks where they are easy to reach. Put rims on pullout trays or shelves to keep things from falling off.

■ Magnetic racks are especially useful for storing knives out of the reach of children.

Getting the Most Out of— And Into—the One-Room Apartment

Single-room apartments, sometimes called studio apartments or "efficiencies," present an enormous challenge to the skill and imagination of the decorator. One room must provide a functional sleeping area, dining area, storage, an entertaining or relaxation spot, perhaps working space, also kitchen and bath. You must plan ahead to combine successfully these everyday activities within the single room.

Begin with a simple sketch of the space available, drawn to scale if possible, and include jogs, extrusions, fireplace extension (if it is there), door swing if inward, and even the space between bottoms of windows and the floor.

A number of essential factors must be considered in the initial stages of planning. Determine how much storage space you will need, where the bed (or sofa bed) is to be placed, the location of the dining table, the potentials of multipurpose furniture. Define your decorating plan.

Essential storage

Neatness in a studio apartment counts. A home that combines comfort, serenity, and attractiveness, though limited in space, is the ultimate goal. So be sure to provide enough storage space to handle all your belongings: clothing, books, records, needlework, pots, pans, wines, and curios. For specifics, check *Storage*, immediately preceding.

After you have assigned a place for everything, housekeeping should be simple. But you must discipline yourself to do it. A one-room flat can look completely disorderly if you leave one day's clothing, one meal's implements, or even a Sunday paper spread about.

Sleeping and seating arrangements

First decide where to place the bed or beds, keeping in mind the kind of bed best suited to the room: a daybed heaped with pillows for daytime seating; a convertible sofa bed that opens at night; or a drop-down, vertically stored model. A more adventurous departure for a small apartment, should it have a very high ceiling, is the sleeping loft, usually constructed of wood about 7 feet above the floor. The space below can be used as a dressing room, closet, or work area.

Sometimes it is best not to buy a bed until you have considered the room layout. The bed belongs where you will be most content sleeping; so check that your bed area has some sense of shelter, is out of drafts, and away from radiators. In most studio apartments the bed doubles for guest seating and you will not want to sabotage your conversational grouping by planning only for sleeping. Some juggling of purposes has to be done and a compromise made.

After you know where the bed will be placed, plan a table arrangement convenient both for the seated guests and for your bedtime use. If a coffee table stands in front of a sofa bed by day, make sure it can be readily moved at night. This is easily accomplished if you use furniture on casters. Check the lighting. This must also be chosen both for entertaining and for bedtime needs—reading in bed, for example.

Placing the dining table

The dining table is another major piece to be considered in the planning stage. It may be a permanent fixture, doubling perhaps as a desk

Elegant and serene, the furnishings in this studio apartment were harmoniously assembled to serve many demands. The black, white, cinnamon color scheme enlarges and links together the varied elements in the room. A dominant white, repeated throughout the apartment, creates an illusion of spaciousness, as do see-through coffee tables that seem to occupy no space at all. By moving the lightweight coffee tables and opening the convertible sofa, a luxurious living room is changed into sleeping quarters. Lighting and end tables serve equally well for entertaining or bedtime use. When not set for meals, the skirted table displays decorative accessories.

or occasional table, or it may be a drop-leaf type that can fit into a closet when not in use, or the type that pulls out of a piece of storage furniture, as do the tables shown on these pages.

Keep in mind accessibility to the cooking area. Your furniture arrangement should allow

A simple cabinet with two bifold doors conceals a 38x104-inch dining table. Leaves to expand the table are stored on the shelf of the cabinet when not in use. For more information about dual-purpose items similar to this one, see *Apartment Living,* Vol. 2, pp. 228 and 230.

This versatile see-through room divider is an excellent build-it-yourself project for apartment dwellers. The divider provides storage space, display area, and a serving shelf—all within a space measuring 7 feet 10 inches in height, 6 feet in width, and 16 inches in depth. The fold-down serving shelf forms a buffet 4 feet 10½ inches long, 18 inches deep. When not in use this shelf functions as a decorative panel. The entire unit consists of 5 basic sections: 4 columns, each slotted to accept glass or plastic shelves, and a cornice. Send for PP 4105-1.

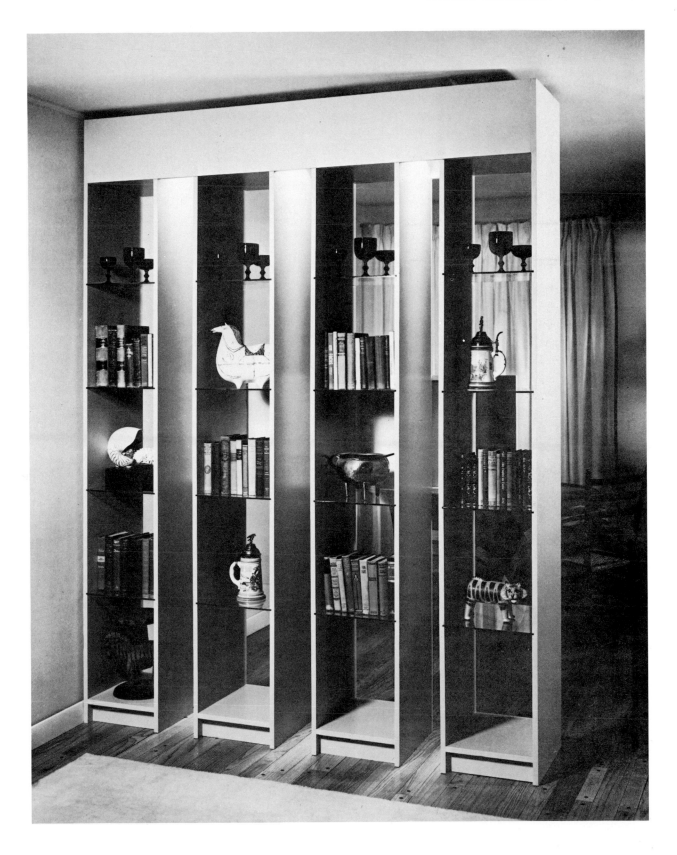

A studio apartment that also serves as a home office has an inviting lived-in appearance and is packed with good ideas for one-room living. A foldaway Murphy bed, indicated in an open position on the plan by a dotted line, folds up, complete with bedding, into a wall cabinet. It can be purchased with the cabinet that stands against the wall, or with only the spring system and a mattress for do-it-yourself carpenters. In this case, a false wall was built along the entire side of the apartment, with a recess for the bed covered by a pair of 24-inch folding doors. Shelves and lighting may be installed above. Another attractive idea employed in the room is the metal bookshelf in the foreground. Originally an assembly of commercial steel shelves and supports more commonly used in warehouses and stockrooms, it was spray-lacquered dark blue to give it a more stylish appearance. Other items that serve a double purpose are an old trunk used both as an end table and as storage for linens and pillow, and a Parsons table that is a desk by day and a dining table at night.

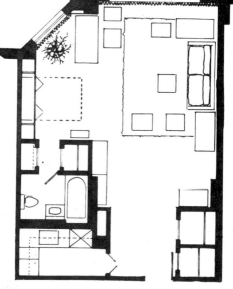

ENTRY

FOYER

BENCH

KITCHEN

LIN.

BATH

DINING

BOOKS

DESK

BOOKS

SOFA

FOLDING BED

BENCH

F./T.V.

LIVING

CONSOLE

This cleverly organized studio apartment has all the comforts and none of the housework of a much larger dwelling. A glance at the floor plan shows how this was accomplished with room to spare by well-thought-out flexible furniture arrangements. The furniture itself was chosen for fine design, portability, and adaptability. For example, twin Parsons tables can be pushed together to form an ample dining table or set end to end for use as a buffet. The folding bed and chairs were good choices for space saving; and the adjustable bookshelves were a fine solution to the inevitable storage problem. Furniture is all in go-with-anything colors. Bright accents are a meld of modern and folk art. All are blended together to form an environment rich in rhythm, spirit, and modern good taste. The result is a perfect habitat for mobile young city dwellers.

a clear traffic lane from the range to the dining table. This is especially important in small areas when a large piece of furniture is used. Some studio-apartment dwellers succeed in seating four or six at an expandable table; others prefer using the table for buffet service, serving on trays or on fold-up individual tables. A supply of small foldaway or stackable guest tables simplifies entertaining.

Dual-purpose furniture

Other items you might consider, in addition to the convertible beds and tables, are storage units that act as room dividers, nestable or stackable tables and benches for parties, collapsible tabletops to use on card tables for din-

ner parties, folding chairs, and roll-about carts. (See *Dual-Purpose Furniture,* Vol. 7, p. 1250.)

Decorating a studio apartment

The rules for decorating a one-room home are not greatly different from those for any other room in terms of scale, color, and furniture style and period. It is wise, however, to remember that you are limited to one room unless you leave home for a breather. Use whatever you know you will appreciate seeing often, and avoid fads unless they are removable. Current posters are great fun for a while, but because of their nature as temporary decorations, do not fix them permanently to the wall; tack or tape them up instead.

Efficient Study Needs
Proper Atmosphere and Equipment

A study area should be an island of quiet, safely removed from the noisy distracting hustle and bustle of daily household routine. The basic requisites of a practical and congenial retreat for studious work and pleasure are a clear surface for writing, a comfortable chair designed for an upright posture, good artificial lighting free of glare and dim spots, and shelf and drawer space to satisfy the user.

Today, paper work and record-keeping are ubiquitous burdens. Books, papers, ballpoint pens, rulers, staplers, checkbook, postage stamps, personalized notepaper, and envelopes are just a few of the items that stock a working desk. Housewives make out budgets, pay bills, and keep appointment calendars; the head of the house maintains tax records and files expense accounts; college students copy notes and type term papers. Even pig-tailed six-year-olds may have arithmetic workbooks to puzzle over at homework time. Everyone in the family needs a study area at some time, and many homes provide more than one.

Space and variations

With an extra room in the house—a den, library, or guest room—you can furnish your study generously with book-lined walls, a spacious desk, and comfortable armchairs that invite an evening of leisurely reading. However, the arrangement of an effective study area does not necessarily require a separate room or luxurious accommodations.

A housewife, alone much of the time in a quiet house, may elect to place an elegant writing table in the living room. Here, relaxed in gracious surroundings, she can make telephone calls, address invitations, or write letters. In a more practical and down-to-earth vein, she may claim a corner of the kitchen for her own, keeping an eye on the cookies baking in the oven while dispatching the numerous paper-work chores of the family. Bedrooms are usually havens of quiet, and thus make excellent sites for study areas.

A student's study area is often a corner of his bedroom; he can simply close the door whenever he wants undisturbed time for study. Brothers or sisters sharing a bedroom can be provided with duplicate desks so each can have his own study area and work at his own assignment or hobby.

Where space is severely limited, as in a one-room studio apartment, the dining table can also function as a desk. Papers and stationery can be stored wherever space is available, or the dining table may be an ingenious double-duty piece with rollaway storage cabinets underneath.

Do not locate a study area in a family room that houses a television set, record player, Ping-Pong table, or card table. The competition from the afternoon bridge club or the evening newscaster is not conducive to good study and work habits. For the obvious reason, avoid foyers and all much-traveled hallways and corridors.

The essentials of a study area, the writing surface or desk and storage drawers and shelves, can be remarkably adaptable. You can align them vertically or horizontally or angle them around a corner to fit existing space requirements. If space is limited and storage needs are great, the desk can be placed at right angles to the wall with shelves behind and beside it to

Prints depicting magnificently war-bonneted American Indians are appropriately combined with a Navaho fabric in a spirited den-study. Desk and chair are typically colonial; so also is a braided rug on a wood-planked floor.

The fabric on far wall and nearer screen panels divides the long room into zones. When the study area is in use, the screen separates it from the living area. A plan such as this would be an efficient solution to a space problem.

create an efficient corner. A wall of books, incidentally, is a splendid insulator of sound, so your study corner itself will contribute to a lower decibel level. When the study area is part of the bedroom, it can be integrated into a wall system that also includes drawer and closet space for clothing, hobby equipment, or toys.

The study fits the task

If the study area is to serve mainly for letter writing and compiling invitation lists, a writing table with shallow drawers is a charming addition to a living room or bedroom. Such a table can be placed in odd-shaped wall jogs, alcoves, or bay window areas. Set beneath a window or against a wall, your writing surface can be accessorized to blend in with the room scheme, featuring decorative desktop items.

The serious student, whose books and papers are his tools, will need shelves on which to store his atlas, dictionary, and textbooks. If, as many modern students do, he owns a typewriter, there should be space for a typewriter table or adequate desktop room for the typewriter in addition to books and papers.

His notebooks and papers are probably inconvenient for study, as well as untidy, when strewn about. In order to organize these loose materials, provide drawers or set cardboard file boxes on open shelves. Cleaning will be much easier if the student has a place for storage and keeps his desk in a relatively orderly condition.

Your eyes at work

Whether it is large and workmanlike or small and elegant, no study is a success unless the il-

Bookcase and bulletin board flank windows that are "blacked out" by sill-length curtains and heavy shades. One end of the desk serves as night table; the other end houses drawer space for clothes. The unit is 9½ feet long, 1½ feet deep, but could be adapted to your needs.

An awkward off-center window is merged into a youngster's bedroom study, creating a delightful corner for doing homework or contentedly reading a book. A home handyman can easily achieve the same effect: the vertical panels above the desk are fastened to a simple framework of three 1x8-inch planks nailed or screwed to the wall; after shelves are installed, add plywood fascia and arches. The desktop is made from a hollow-core door.

ows. If the light source is a lamp, it should be placed to the left side for a right-handed person, and to the right side for a left-handed person. Fluorescent lamps have the advantage of being a cool light source; incandescent lamps light a wider area and are generally available in styles offering more variety and flexibility. Wall-hung or ceiling-hung lamps are convenient when desktop space is limited.

A country bumpkin, a shy belle, and a pair of curious bluebirds were painted above a little girl's desk. The desk itself, set between a pair of old chests, was the work of a home handyman. First, plastic laminate was bonded to the side and three edges of a piece of ¾-inch plywood. Four strap-iron tabs were then bent and screwed to the top, which was set in place between the chests. The desk can be easily adapted to different decorating schemes as the girl grows.

lumination is correctly planned. Good lighting completely eliminates the possibility of eyestrain. Lamps and lighting fixtures are much more than decorative accessories, and they should be chosen and placed for optimal results.

Strong contrasts of light and dark lead to eye fatigue, so avoid creating a pool of light from a desk lamp in an otherwise unlighted room. For the same reason, do not choose a stark white blotter for a dark desktop. The contrast may be a dramatic decorative accent, but it is much harder on the eyes than paler colors, for example a soft pastel green or medium blue.

Do not use high-intensity lamps for regular desk lighting; these miniature spotlights are valuable for special occasions when very fine work is underway, but their light is too brilliant and too strong for use during prolonged reading or writing. Place your light so it throws no shad-

The treasures of a teenage boy—camera equipment, a portable television set, a musical instrument—as well as books, papers, school supplies, and clothing—are all accommodated by an 8-foot-long desktop of laminated plastic with drawers below and shelf and cabinet storage above. The molded-plastic chair moves on large casters.

The right accessories

Some people take pride and pleasure in the look of a bare, unadorned desktop. Most, however, are less ascetic, and they have a choice of desk accessories that run the gamut from practical and functional items to whimsical, sentimental, and elegant ones. Handsome desk accessories are available in matched tooled-leather sets that include blotter, letter holder, pencil holder, photograph frame, and wastepaper basket. Such sets are particularly suitable for a man's desk.

Both of those necessary modern devices, the telephone and the typewriter, are now available

Twin study areas are stretched along the wall of a boys' bedroom. Duplicate desk-and-chest units can be puchased at store or lumberyard with hardware for connecting, then finished at home. Lumberyards also cut 1x6-inch boards for shelves, to be hung with 1-inch laths, shelf strips, and brackets. Curtain-rod finials, cut in half, top off the strips.

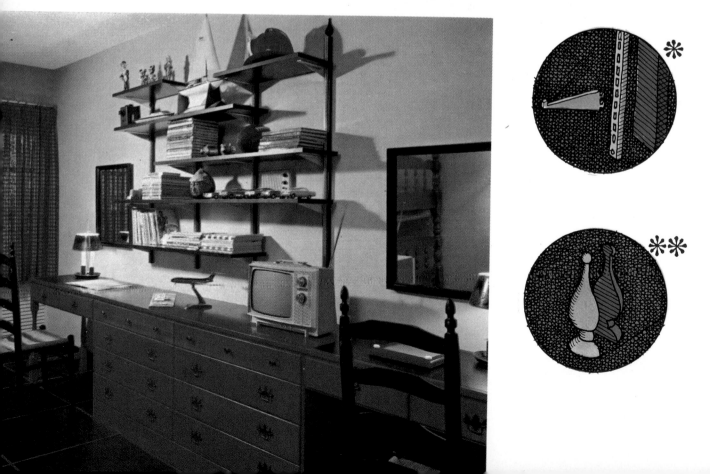

in decorator colors, and telephones can be purchased in models that feature antique charm or push-button efficiency.

Daily calendars and appointment diaries are popular desktop accessories, and they can be selected to provide an appropriate decorative accent. Lucite or metal bookholders make useful and attractive research aids; they keep reading material in place and free the hands of the reader for taking notes or checking references.

Desk accessories can be custom-made at home to coordinate with a room scheme. Glue fabric remnants onto frozen-juice cans, and use these "upholstered" containers on the desktop for paper clips, rubber bands, or pencils. Or use Victorian shaving mugs to hold pens and pencils and combine them with a miniature chest of drawers that stores stationery and postage stamps. Screw a pencil sharpener into an inconspicuous corner of a bookshelf, or invest in a sharpener with suction-cup adhesion to avoid drilling in shelves of fine wood. Often, second-hand stores and thrift shops reveal odd items that are perfect for use on a desktop.

A small dining table converts handily to a desk, a double-duty arrangement that is more than welcome in close quarters. Desk drawers and files are separate units and serve as couch-side tables when dining is in progress. When it is time for writing or study, the units slide into place. Hinged flip-top at left provides typewriter space.

A drop-leaf table with one leaf removed provides a sturdy and convenient writing surface in a country-style living room. The desk does double duty as a table during parties. The Chinese-red chair and pink blotter are vivid accents supplementing the vibrant color dashes on matching wallpaper and draperies. Lack of storage is only difficulty.

How to Cut Back on Sunlight On Your Open Areas

Even the most avid sun worshipper will admit that there can be too much of a good thing as he seeks a shady spot on a midsummer day. Erecting a roof or screen to block or filter out the sun's direct rays from a portion of your outdoor living area gives you a choice between sun and shade. You might place such a screen so that it admits the morning sun but blocks it out when it is directly overhead. Or you might prefer a roof of solid material (translucent plastic, perhaps) that will not only filter out the sunlight but will also provide shelter from a sudden rainstorm. An appropriately placed screen can also serve to shield the patio from uncomfortably brisk breezes.

Architectural considerations

Properly planned, a sun filter can be an important architectural asset to your house. For example, if the house is relatively small and disproportionately high, the addition of a patio roof continuing the roof line of the main structure may make it appear longer, lower, and much better balanced; or you may be able to combine the patio area with a carport or a storage area for lawn, garden, and terrace equipment.

You can add visual interest to the house as well as to the patio with a sun roof or screen of wood louvers, slats, or latticework. This will create a fascinating and constantly changing shadow pattern. Some patterned plastic panels produce similar effects.

To help you visualize your finished sun filter while you are still in the planning stage, photograph the outdoor living area from several different angles—black-and-white Polaroid pictures are fine. Then use a black grease pencil to sketch in the proposed structure. Try several different versions, keeping in mind the position of the sun at the time of day you want the patio protected from its rays.

An important aesthetic consideration is that the structure should relate in some way to the house itself, even though it may be unattached and some distance away from the house. You can establish this relationship in a number of ways. Similar roof configurations may do it, as could the use of similar materials. A common trim color for both house and sun roof or screen is another good tie-in feature.

One word of caution here: before you go too far in planning any structure to shield your outdoor living area, check your local building codes. There may be limitations on the type of structure you can erect, for example; or restrictions on how close you can build to your property line.

Choice of materials

For a slatted sun filter, use 1x3s, 1x4s, or 2x4s —the dimension will depend on the type of construction and the spans to be covered by the boards. If you plan to paint the boards, do so before assembly; if they are spaced fairly close together, painting could be a problem later on. If you prefer to leave them unfinished, use red-

If your terrace is bordered by lush garden growth as is the one shown, consider extending your sun roof over the garden as well if the plants and flowers are shade-tolerant. Post-and-beam construction is used here, with intermediate structural members of butt-joined 2x8s. Between these are sections of removable reed matting to provide shade where and when you may want it. Remember that coverings that keep out rain require that you water plants instead of depending on rainfall.

wood because it is highly resistant to damage from exposure. After a few years, it will weather to a mellow silvery gray.

A louvered filter can be built of 1x6s or 1x8s. Finishing procedures are the same as above. Exterior-grade plywood can also be used for louvers, especially if you prefer wider ones.

If your plans call for large sections of the structure to block out the sun completely (a partial roof, for example), plywood is again the choice. If you do build a roof, cover it with the same roofing material that was used on your house. A screen made of plywood provides privacy as well as blocking out sun and wind. It can be painted in bright, decorative colors.

Translucent fiber glass and plastic panels are widely favored for patio roofs and screens. The strong rigid panels cut down heat and glare but admit soft diffused light. They are available in a wide range of colors and textures.

There are both flat and corrugated translucent panels. The latter type provides reasonable ri-gidity over a fairly great span so that the panels can cover large areas with a minimum of wood or metal framing.

Many other materials can be used for your sun filter. Consider bamboo, or reed matting; or mix and match materials. Your choice is as broad as your imagination.

Types of construction

Post-and-beam construction is favored for most types of sun filters. If the structure is attached to the house, use sturdy lag bolts to fasten a 2x6 plate to the house studs, then build out from there. Roof pitch should be figured at a minimum of ½ inch per foot.

For a large freestanding structure, footings should be poured below the frost line before the supporting posts are set in concrete. Smaller screens are built in the same way as fences. The supporting posts are either embedded in concrete or simply placed in tamped earth on a bed of gravel to allow for drainage.

Ever-changing patterns of sunlight filter through this sun screen covering a large portion of an attached outdoor living room. Double 2x10 beams, painted black for design emphasis, support the evenly spaced 2x3 slats. The garage wall at right is blended into the scheme with a disguising trellis of 1x1s nailed to 1x2 crosspieces. Projecting 3 feet beyond the end of the garage, this trellis effectively screens garage doors and much activity from the patio.

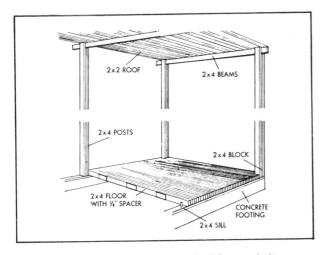

This smartly styled and simple-to-build sun shelter provides shade and seclusion where you need it. Materials used are inexpensive and blend with almost any style of architecture. Length is determined by the amount of space available, but width should not exceed 6 feet—otherwise the structure may be unstable. Concrete footings along each side support a floor of 2x4s laid on edge, with ⅛-inch spacing between. Posts are formed of two 2x4s, with a 2x4-block spacer between. At the top, 2x4 beams are sandwiched between the double posts. With the framing erected, 2x2 slats are nailed at regular intervals across the beams. The sun screen is assembled of evenly spaced 2x2s nailed to two horizontal 2x4s, which are then bolted to the upright posts.

It follows that, if you do a lot of living and dining outdoors, you would enjoy an outdoor kitchen. This one-wall cooking center shares shelter space with a grouping of dining furniture—the entire unit measures 12x24 feet, but the size can, of course, be adapted to your own needs. The kitchen features a built-in barbecue, sink, undercounter refrigerator, and storage space for barbecue gear, pottery,

glasses, trays, and other table-setting needs. The work counter is big enough to double as a buffet top or snack-and-drink center. To protect the outdoor chef from the heat of the sun, a simple structure is provided. 4x4 supporting posts are set into concrete; beams are 2x6s, supporting the 2x4 rafters. 1x2 slats are laid flat across the rafters with equal spacing between boards.

Create a Sunshine Haven Used Around the Year

Some families call it the morning room; to others, it is the summer living room; still others refer to it as an open-air parlor. By any name, the sun porch can be one of the most delightful and relaxing areas of your home.

Sun porches take many forms. They are often found in older homes as simple glass-enclosed rooms at either front or rear. Some homes boast "solaria," usually separated from the living room or dining room by French doors. Many newer homes have sun rooms that are extensions of the living or family rooms; the sun rooms in turn open onto terraces or other outdoor living areas.

In any form, the advantages of such a room are many. Because it is glass-enclosed, it allows you to enjoy the sun and the outdoor view, even during the cooler parts of the day—and of the year as well. Fitted with screens, the porch offers a pleasant sitting area for the warm seasons, admitting cooling breezes while keeping out the insect pests that abound in summertime. And if heating is provided for the area you can use it year-round, on all but the very coldest winter days.

Minor adjustments

If your home does not already have a sun porch, you will probably discover many opportune ways of creating one by working with existing arrangements. Perhaps you have an open porch; enclosing it, or a part of it, is a relatively easy matter. Usually, all that is involved is removing the porch railing and installing full-height window units. A doorway must be provided, of course, but in most cases no major structural work need be done.

You might enclose a breezeway between house and garage or house and carport. With sidewalls and roof already in place, this process also is a relatively simple one. Floor-to-ceiling window and door units at front and rear will do the job. Slding glass doors are often preferred for such an installation.

A carport itself may be enclosed to become a sun porch. Here again, the major structural work is already in place, and all you have to do is to put up the walls of glass and screening. In some instances, you may wish to raise a floor that is several steps below the floor level of the house.

Other areas of your home that might lend themselves for conversion to a sun porch are the entryways and the patio. If these are already roofed over, enclosing them is simple, as noted above. If not, a post-and-beam framework can be erected to support a roof. The roof itself can match that of the house, or you may prefer to cover it with a translucent fiber glass or plastic material that will diffuse the sun's glare while admitting its light and warmth. With the roof in place, install the window walls and enjoy your new sun room.

A sunny room, right, was once an open entryway. When the area was enclosed and the double entrance doors moved to the new wall, the resultant interior space became a year-round morning room with a bright outlook onto the garden and the day. In the window wall, a side door was provided for direct access to yard and garden. The original brick floor of the entry was retained; it points up the outdoor feeling of the new room and is durable and easily maintained. Large glass areas have to be shielded in regions where the sun can be merciless; here, fadeproof cotton draperies, hung with wooden rings on poles, can be drawn to subdue the fieriest days.

Planning a new sun porch

If your home offers none of the above possibilities for a sun-porch conversion, give some careful thought to the question of where you would like to build a new porch. Ideally, it should be oriented to catch the morning sun—having your first cup of coffee while soaking up the warmth of the early sunlight somehow makes the whole day ahead seem brighter. The porch should open off one of the living areas of the house: living room, family room, dining room, or kitchen, although a private sun porch can be located off the master bedroom. In the latter case, plan to provide privacy by erecting a barrier screen or planting trees or high bushes.

Take into account the views that your lot has to offer. Given a choice between looking at

A seldom-used open porch was converted into the airy summer living room shown here. Screening provides protection from insects and a welcome flow of balmy breezes. A roof of the same screening makes this truly a sun room, capturing the outdoors in full measure. The cement floor is covered with weather-resistant outdoor-indoor carpeting; contemporary metal and nylon-mesh furniture also withstands sun and showers. Lush plantings and a small reflecting pool complete the garden setting. A corner door leads to the backyard

Pattern helps turn a sun porch into a second living room. With walls of glass as a background, you can go all out with bold stripes or brightly colored florals. The room is furnished with slimly scaled pieces that are quite in tune with a light and informal atmosphere, and the sprightly stripe at the windows and on the sofas sets a cheerful mood. Tieback draperies are colorful without lessening sunlight; wood-slat blinds can be lowered for light control and privacy. The wrought-iron furniture, campaign chair, and wicker chest contribute to the room's airy quality; fence conceals neighbor's backyard.

your garden or your neighbor's driveway, you will almost certainly opt for the former, even though other considerations may have to be sacrificed. Before making any decision, draw a rough sketch of your property, showing the placement of the house; include locations of trees, walks, gardens, and the like (you can trace your map from the plot survey that was made when you bought or built your home). Study the plan carefully; you can probably arrive at a satisfactory compromise that balances the claims of proper orientation and pleasing view.

When you have a good idea of what you want to build, check your local building code and zoning ordinances. If the sun porch is to be near the lot line, you will probably have to observe a minimum-setback requirement. There may also be restrictions as to the type of addition you can make to your home, including regulations such as minimum sizes for rooms and heights of ceilings. Many municipalities require that you file for a building permit and submit detailed plans of any proposed construction.

Building your sun porch

The construction of your new sun porch will most likely depend on the type of construction used to build the existing house. Generally, it is preferable to set the porch floor level with the house floor. If the house is built on a concrete slab, you will probably want to have a slab poured for the porch, too. If the house has a basement or crawl space, you can build foundation walls for the porch and install conventional joists and subflooring.

Walls can be of either standard stud framing or heavier post-and-beam construction. If you build a conventional shingle roof, match the shingles as closely as possible to those of the house; continue the roof line of the house, or set the porch roof at a complementary angle. If you wish to invite maximum light and warmth into your sun porch, consider a translucent roof of fiber glass or plastic.

Sturdy low-maintenance materials are favored for this informal room. The floor may be covered with indoor-outdoor carpet or easy-to-clean tiles. The finishing materials can also serve to tie the sun porch to adjacent areas. For example, if the porch opens onto a wood deck, it might feature a floor of the same wood. If there is a patio beyond, both areas might share a floor of brick or flagstone. If the sun porch is off the family room, the beamed ceiling of the family room can be repeated over the porch. Or you can panel the house wall of the sun porch to match the paneling in the family room.

Lighting the sun porch

Despite its name, you will probably use your sun porch as much during the hours after dark

A sun porch serves the family as a year-round combination sitting room and informal dining room. Baseboard heating, plus the double-glazed windows, keeps things cozy during the colder months; carpeting and underfloor insulation also help. During warmer weather, the lower portions of the windows are opened to catch the cool breezes. A hardwood-strip ceiling complements informal country furnishings. A key to the enjoyment of this porch is the view outside; the homeowner invested considerable effort in attractive landscaping.

as you do when the sun is providing light. There-fore, good lighting is important. To a certain extent, you can light the sun porch according to standards that apply to other rooms in the house. For example, soft indirect lighting is fine for conversation areas, but more powerful and direct light is needed for reading. But you must also consider factors unique to a room of this kind. Windows and screening provide little of the light reflection that helps to create an indoor room's level of illumination.

Generally, one or more ceiling fixtures or hanging lamps should be installed for good over-all illumination. Supplement this lighting with reading lamps strategically placed alongside the most comfortable chairs; these will provide a softer effect than similar indoor lighting, but should be more than adequate for the porch.

Heating for year-round use

Even if your sun porch is built over an open crawl space, it can be heated for year-round use. In such a situation, of course, the area beneath the floor should first be well insulated. Electric heating units are generally used for such installations, although it may sometimes be feas-ible to tap into the central heating unit. Where electric baseboard units are planned, be sure to allow enough space beneath the windows to accommodate the baseboards.

Combined with earth-toned pottery on a sawbuck table, a bowl of fresh-scrubbed vegetables makes an attractive centerpiece in the relaxed setting of a rustic screened porch. The atmosphere is enhanced by a sturdy old-brick floor and an antique dry sink full of freshly cut flowers from the garden. The porch offers all the delight of dining in the open air plus protection from insects.

Because of its controlled climate, a sun porch is an ex-cellent spot for growing plants. Here, despite snow out-side, plants indoors are flourishing. This sun porch was created by remodeling a section of the existing living room; glassing it in, adding an electric heating unit, laying a slate floor, and installing a small sunken pool in the bay window. The room was left open to the living room.

The transition between indoors and outdoors should be natural and easy, and you can accomplish this by using design and materials to unify areas. A combination screened porch and deck features overhead beams that form a sun shield for part of the deck. Underfoot, wood decking runs uninterrupted indoors and out. The porch serves as an open-air family room and dining area when weather is nice. Inexpensive slat blinds provide protection from afternoon sun; hanging fixtures give adequate light for all porch and deck activities.

A Basic Roundup on Choosing And Building Your New Pool

If you wish to avoid the discomforts and long traffic-jammed hours of leading summer caravans to crowded public beaches and swimming pools, perhaps you are ready to join the more than 750,000 American families that enjoy the pleasures of home in-ground pools, or the 3,000,000 or so that have purchased the above-ground type. Today, building your own quality pool requires less time and money than ever before, and the savings to be gained in buying premanufactured pools place this former luxury facility within reach of many home-owners' budgets.

It is the sheer love of swimming that decides most families on pool ownership; along with the fun, you will appreciate your pool for its many important contributions to active living: increased physical fitness, the chance to swim in unpolluted waters, privacy and convenience for the whole family, and the safest possible environment for all water sports.

Begin by composing a mental image of inviting blue water under a sunny sky; then give careful thought to the various technical and personal considerations, and work out the best installation for your home and family. When completed, your pool will take you through the coming seasons with a maximum of refreshment.

Locating your pool

The location of your pool is a matter of primary importance. Planning with your aesthetic preferences in mind, an experienced builder will be able to help you with your site selection. He can also point out any local building, zoning, and health ordinances that impose site, construction, or drainage requirements.

Experts recommend that a pool be situated on or near the highest point in the yard, thus preventing debris from draining into the water.

A concern for safety suggests that the pool be located in the immediate vicinity of the house, where swimmers, and most especially young children, will always be clearly visible from the inside.

The swimming day, and the whole season as well, will be perceptibly lengthened if the pool is given a southern exposure. This orientation always assures you of maximum warmth for swimming and poolside activities. A shaded area close by the pool is desirable because you will frequently enjoy relaxing out of the heat.

It is convenient for swimmers if the dash from the pool to the inside shower is a short one. If it is arranged so they can come in directly, without crossing through the living room or dining room, you will more easily preserve the neatness of these areas.

You should allow plenty of room near the pool for lounging or sunning since more time will be spent out of the water than in it. Space for outdoor entertaining is welcome; in most cases, planning the pool around a patio or sun deck is a very convenient and satisfying arrangement.

Create an oasis

Appropriate landscaping is the best means of bringing your pool to life as a gracious and comfortable family and social setting. Suitable plants will provide "air conditioning" and shade, privacy, color, a formal or contemporary theme, and also tie in your pool neatly with house and yard. If possible, trees and shrubbery that shed

A kidney-shaped pool situated close to the house is an excellent example of good planning. Pool blends in with its surroundings and offers swimmers quick and easy access to rear of the house. There is also ample room around the pool for lounging, and tall leaf-shedding trees are far enough away so leaves do not fall into water.

leaves, as well as flowering plants that attract insects, should be located away from the pool for the sake of a clean surface.

Maintenance will be easier with raised planting beds, which should be buttressed with a solid edge to protect the water from leaves and debris. A lawn next to the pool means grass cuttings in the water or tracked in the house by wet feet; between beds and shrubs you might intersperse a low-growing ground cover such as ivy.

Size, shape, and cost

The number of pool shapes that are available to the would-be owner is virtually unlimited.

In addition to the familiar rectangle, you can request a round pool, a kidney shape, an oval, L and S shapes, or a free-form pool. In most cases, pools are custom-built to suit a family's taste, pocketbook, and property. The smallest practical pool that is recommended measures 12x27 feet, and the most popular size range, chosen by some 85 percent of all buyers, varies from 15x30 to 20x40 feet; such a pool is large enough to accommodate all water activities.

Prices go from about $200 for the least expensive above-ground pool to more than $10,000 for a luxurious in-ground facility. The larger above-ground pools start at about $2,000.

Materials and installation

After deciding on the size and shape of your pool, you must make a selection from among the various materials available for construction. Permanent in-ground pools of virtually any shape are available in all of the materials discussed in the following list:

- *Poured concrete.* A traditional pool type constructed by pouring concrete into forms to mold the walls and floor. Pools of this type are very strong and long-lasting, even in areas where difficulties are caused by natural factors of soil and drainage. Prices range from $3,500 to $8,000.

- *Sprayed concrete.* Also referred to by the trade name Gunite, this type of construction is quite popular because of the strong seamless structure it produces and the ease with which it is molded into elegant shapes. Under high pressure, the concrete is sprayed over a mesh framework; the surface is then smoothed and

A heated year-round pool is flanked on three sides by the house, and by shutters at its far end. This private 16x30-foot pool features a redwood apron around the borders. Sliding glass doors provide a fascinating year-round view of pool.

Contemporary is the word for a wide-roof pool house centered in front of the pool. The house offers dressing rooms for the quick-change convenience of the swimming brigade and kitchen facilities for barbecues.

painted or covered with plaster. Gunite pools range in cost between $5,000 and $8,000.

■ *Vinyl liner.* This colorful and relatively inexpensive in-ground pool is constructed by placing a tough waterproof vinyl liner over walls of concrete block, wood, aluminum, fiber glass, or steel. The liner can be torn or punctured, but it is also quite easy to repair. Prices go from $3,000 to $4,500.

■ *Fiber glass.* Sections of strong plastic are put together with concrete footings and metal supports to form a very contemporary pool that is highly resistant to climate and chemicals. Prices range from $6,000 to $7,000.

■ *Brick.* The use of brick masonry reinforced by vertical and horizontal steel rods results in a pool that is beautiful but expensive.

The installation of any in-ground pool is considered a property improvement, so you can expect an increase in your taxes. Above-ground pools are not subject to property taxes because they are portable and can either be sold with the house or moved with the family.

Above-ground pools are generally constructed by placing a vinyl liner over wood, steel, or aluminum supports, with a decking of wood. For diving you will require a dug-out portion at one end, called a hopper. An above-ground pool can be quickly and easily installed by the homeowner himself.

Equipment and safety
Today, many pools are sold complete with filter and pump, diving board, underwater light,

leaf skimmer, life preserver, and ladder. If they are not included in the original installation, all of this equipment can be purchased separately. Among other accessories designed to make things easier for the pool owner are such items as a water heater, a pool cover that can support two adults, a pole and ring buoys for use during emergencies, and chemicals that purify the water. Enthusiasts who want to extend the swimming season indefinitely can enclose their pools with inflatable-dome covers. This can be expensive since a compressor may be required to keep the dome inflated; for larger pools the price can exceed $1,000.

Your ordinances may not so require, but it is always recommended that you entirely sur-round your pool with a solid fence at least 5 feet high. This will prevent small children in your neighborhood from getting into the water when your family is away from home.

You can buy a floating pool alarm that will signal you and the neighbors whenever the water is unexpectedly invaded. Simply activate this device when the pool is to be left unattended.

Have the pool's electrical equipment checked regularly for possible corrosion due to the chemicals in the water. Use only battery-powered appliances in the pool area, which should be free of electric outlets.

Pool maintenance

It used to be that cleaning a pool was a bothersome chore. It had to be emptied on a regular basis and then scrubbed and refilled. Today's pools are great time-savers as they are equipped with recirculating filters that automatically remove impurities and permit the water to be reused safely over long periods of time. The maintenance required by most home pools averages only from 1½ to 4 hours of work per week.

An averaging-all-costs estimate that includes chemical treatment, repair, and replacement of equipment prices maintenance over a 10-year period at an average near $200 per year. Automatic chemical feeders and cleaning devices are available for those who wish to be entirely free of pool chores, or you can have your pool maintained by a service company or by your builder-dealer. Under a contract arrangement, the cost of such service ranges from $20 to $70 per month depending on pool size and the care specified. In addition to standard maintenance and regular on-site inspections, the service operation can also include opening the pool in spring and winterizing it in the autumn, eliminating maintenance worries from the recreation picture.

This terrace contains both pool and a patio above it. A juniper hedge and grape-stake fence outline the terrace and give privacy to pool and surrounding area.

Unusual use of mirrors between wooden latticework panels accents this pool. Marking the boundary of the property, the panel-mirror section shown contributes visual interest and a spacious look to a small area.

Choosing a contractor

When you have decided to buy a pool with specific equipment, it is time to bring in a contractor. You can be referred to reliable contractors by banks or the Better Business Bureau, and you can take the advice of neighborhood families who are pleased with their own recently constructed pools. When you shop for a contractor, it is wise to look for one who is affiliated with the National Swimming Pool Institute. Such a builder will offer a standard contract that covers every item in a complete pool package. He will also adhere to the highest standards of workmanship. As well as listing the specifications of all components and pool materials, the contract that you sign should include these provisions:

■ All accessories that the builder will install and their prices, including labor charges.

■ A heater adequate to the size of your pool (if you are installing a heater).

■ The relocation of water, gas, and electrical lines if necessary.

■ Your withholding of part or all of the last payment until the pool is complete and operating.

Above-ground pools that use filtration equipment should include for the given price handrails, filter, chlorinator, test kit, and sand.

You can secure a bond from the builder that guarantees the completion of your pool before a given date, but be sure that you give him enough time to do a good job.

A word of caution: most pool builders are professional businessmen who are anxious to do a first-rate job for you. However, because of the boom in the home swimming pool market, a number of fraudulent operators have invaded the field. Here is a list of traps you should avoid:

■ Never negotiate with a salesman whose credentials you have not checked. Unauthorized salesmen sometimes get people to sign pool contracts and then sell them to the lowest bidder.

■ Never sign a check made out to an individual or give a salesman cash in lieu of a check paid to the company.

This spacious swimming pool is situated conveniently near the house, making its dressing and cooking facilities available for poolside entertaining. The attractive pebbled apron around the pool provides a safe, nonslip surface around the pool's edge.

Four winners. These four handsome pools won in their respective residential categories in a national swimming pool design competition. The dogleg pool with vinyl liner, top left, is one of many designs available to pool buyers.

A gazebo highlights the free-form concrete pool at upper right. The wading pool, at bottom left, punctuates free-form pool. The oval brick pool, bottom right, is enhanced by an enclosed patio house.

■ Never sign a blank contract. Many people do, to their great financial regret.

■ Beware of the salesman who promises to save you money by helping to build your pool. He is probably taking secret rebates from the materials suppliers.

Facts on finance

During the process of planning your pool, the question arises of how to finance it. Approximately half of all the pools built each year are financed through personal loans or home-improvement loans. Money is also made available to would-be pool owners by savings and loan associations, mortgage lenders, insurance companies, or through the pool builder himself. Make sure that you and your builder have agreed on a price before you make a loan so that you will not require additional money later on.

Planning your pool well in advance of construction makes it possible to effect a saving, as there are bargain seasons for pools that vary

Prefabricated pool with turquoise-tinted Krene vinyl liner is inexpensive and need never be drained. Once excavation is completed, pool is relatively easy to assemble.

according to where you live. For example, if you reside in the East or Northeast, you can save money by installing your pool in late summer or early fall. The best buying time for families who live in the South or West is in the winter, particularly in January.

Insurance

Insurance is a must. While a swimming pool may be covered by a homeowner's policy at no extra charge, experts recommend that you get at least

Classically proportioned pool and patio are well integrated with house and garden. Broad steps offer sunbathing space while emphasizing horizontal lines of house; sliding glass doors open directly onto patio from living room.

$100,000 worth of additional insurance. The smart homeowner will carry at least $300,000 in coverage, and this added protection is well worth the few extra dollars spent on annual premiums.

Good living with a pool

Your new pool will be a vital center for every type of family activity from children's fun to adult evening parties, with or without swimming. You will think of numerous ways to enhance the pool setting and increase the convenience of poolside living. Cabanas or a bathhouse for dressing and showering are welcome practical additions, and poolside kitchen facilities will keep mealtimes from interrupting family gatherings on light summer evenings. With patio chairs and tables, a charcoal grill, and perhaps even a sauna bath, you will find yourself in the midst of a private waterside resort that contributes year after year to your family's health, happiness, and spirit of togetherness.

An above-ground installation offers a large pool at low cost. Only excavation needed is in the diving area. Pools of this kind are not taxed since they can be dismantled and moved with the family—or sold with the house.

TABLES

An Historical Survey From
The Ancients to the Most Modern

For centuries table design has been dictated by man's most eccentric social habits. From the ivory-faced game tables of Tutankhamen, 1,500 years before Christ, to today's status cocktail table (often euphemistically referred to as "coffee"), tables have revealed more about manners than any other furnishings, even chairs or beds. Dressing, or vanity, tables were the rage of the Louis courts; tea tables were favored during Queen Anne's reign. Writing tables swept the parlors of Georgian days and no fashionable man or woman was without one. Card tables were an essential of American society of the early 1800s, when both men and women gambled at such games as whist, loo, and faro.

Each major culture has produced its own characteristic table or tables. The 18th-Dynasty Egyptians—the earliest small tables, or stands, in marquetry (combined inlay and veneer) were primarily used to raise such things as knucklebone games from the ground. The eighth-century B.C. Greeks—small tables of bronze and marble, or wood, pushed under a couch when not in use. The early Romans—small round tables with animal legs, sometimes made of marble or silver, and often of citrus wood, convenient as low stands or low seats. Renaissance Italians gave us the folding table that could be set up in whatever room was found convenient. The Moor-dominated Spanish contributed the mosaic-inlaid low "ratona," companion to a cushion-strewn dais, and the brazier, or cooking table. The Japanese—the low armrest table still in use today; the sixteen-century Germans—the big dining tables consisting of a board on trestles, removed after a meal. The English popularized the sewing table, tea table, butler's

tray table, and individual candlestand. Colonial Americans invented the butterfly dining table; contemporary Americans, the Parsons.

Table buffs can name over 3,000 different styles, and cite histories dating back thousands of years. Among the most eccentric and obscure: the Jacobean monk's bench that turns into a table when the back is tilted down over its arms; the gentleman's social table with revolving cylindrical wine-bottle holder; Thomas Jefferson's polygonal table that holds music for five musicians; the gentleman's dressing table, or shaving table, with provisions for a basin, bottles, and other toilet equipment. But even nonbuffs can appreciate and easily recognize the styles in these pages, ranging from essentially beautiful to beautifully essential.

Dining tables
Dining tables as we know them rarely existed outside of Arthurian or other courts until the late seventeenth century, and were generally wood planks supported by temporary trestles and covered with fabric such as linen or velvet. Sit-down social dining was practically unheard of, although formality ran the gamut from reclining dining in early Greek times—when guests lay around huge circular, or semicircular, tables on couches, chairs, and beds—to stand-up dining at the groaning-board feasts in medieval dining halls and, much later, to stand-up brunching at elegant English hunt breakfasts. Until seventeenth-century England, in fact, there were no forks or table-service knives; until the eighteenth century, few plates for individual use. People ate from common bowls, and with their fingers.

Long, heavy tables with six or eight legs connected by square-sectioned stretchers became common throughout the sixteenth and seventeenth centuries; their use was confined to large dining halls of colleges or city companies. Smaller extending tables were used in wealthier homes, allowing dinner parties to be more relaxed and convivial, with the host and hostess at either end of the table and guests along the sides. Until the back stool was invented, late in the 16th century, everyone sat on benches or joint stools.

Today's conception of dining relates table with chairs, as well as other furnishings, and to the space set aside for dining. Homeowners with formal dining rooms to call their own can indulge in the grander styles of tables that accommodate sumptuous banquets. Apartment dwellers can have an equally grand feeling even without equivalent room space. Apartment-sized dining tables are designed for tête-à-tête or tea-for-two proportions, but generally are supplied

The trestle table has survived the centuries since Tudor and Jacobean times to renew the past with its rugged beauty in a contemporary home. Immensely serviceable, its trestle base permits seating to be tucked in under, off-duty. Here, seating is facing benches, or back stools. A pedestal-style tea table, tucked in a corner, holds before-and after-dinner drinks. In the opposite corner: a serving cart, indispensable to the servantless modern scene.

with extra leaves for extending in party situations. Space-shy people often prefer a drop-leaf style that looks so splendid in repose, tucked against a wall. Hardly noticeable between meals, its magic is in its leaves, which lift on cue to greet and seat as many as six people. Another ingenious space-saver is the gregarious round table, particularly on a pedestal, or legless base, much less formidable in a dining "L" or alcove than a conventional square or rectangle. Something about the very roundness seems to save space and to include people in sociable conversation, as opposed to the sometimes inhibiting propriety of being aligned in facing rows.

A dining table in a dining room

Although modern America has a large "snack school" of diners, most people insist on a recog-

nizable dining area, and prefer an actual room. To many, dining without a dining table is like sleeping without a bed. Dining involves much more than just the act of eating: it involves enjoying good food in pleasant surroundings, either alone or in the society of family and friends. Eating in a dining room removes you from the sights and sounds of food preparation, out of the working area, and into a more relaxed and attractive atmosphere. Today's dining rooms can also serve second and third functions as music rooms, art galleries, hobby rooms, salons, or even family boardrooms where people sometimes assemble just to talk and visit. If a dining room is well planned, it does not have to be wasted space that sits darkened and neglected as though off limits except at meal times. Good lighting is important; ample elbowroom, color, and visual interest count high. Materials such as impervious synthetic table surfaces, processed upholstery, soil-resistant flooring or carpeting can turn the most formal room into leisure living space.

A big dining table is reassuring. It can be a baronial slab of invincible oak, or a large round pedestal type with lots of legroom. It can be any period or style, from trestle-based Tudor to Louis XVI with marquetry top, all available in processed or protective finishes. And even

Coffee tables came into their own in the middle of the ▶ seventeenth century, with the increase of social tea-, coffee-, and chocolate-drinking, and the advent of more comfortable (upholstered) seating. Like all good multi-purpose designs, this one also has wide shallow drawers that collect miscellany such as playing cards, coasters, matches, and napkins, and offers the twentieth-century practical bonus of an impervious, leather-looking, inset top. Here, drop-leaf tables double as end tables.

The Parsons table, a modern classic, here is lacquered in a compatible cocoa color and surrounded by modern laminated bentwood side chairs with X-base framing that dates back to the Egyptians. The table can be extended with the addition of two 12-inch apron leaves.

some of the best, woodiest-looking tabletops are plastic, detectable only by the tap instead of thud made by rapping your knuckle against it.

Occasional tables

For thousands of years, until fairly recently, tables have consistently taken an ignominious last place on man's list of home-furnishings needs. Chests, or coffers, in which to store, hoard, and transport treasures, food, and clothes; stools or benches to sit on; and beds to sleep in far outranked all but the merest occasional table. In its turn, the merest occasional table was of far more importance than any other kind, largely because it was lightweight, small-scaled, and movable from room to room, castle to castle, country to country. The most popular and useful occasional tables were low stands to hold games, or long low rectangles used as armrests or as writing, and occasional eating, surfaces when people sat around on the floor or ground. Later, candlestands became popular.

Two particular centuries produced the most ingenious advances in occasional-table designs:

This traditional console table is in the style of George Hepplewhite, London cabinetmaker of the late eighteenth century. Hepplewhite characteristics are the small, light look, slender, tapered legs, concave corners.

A corner table, this one of molded fiber glass does more than just hold things. It articulates space and helps relate bench and sofa seating to each other, rounding off angles, forming a continuous line.

Ceramic tile snack table is a 36-inch circle of ¾-inch plywood attached to one refinished leg of an old table—a wonderful tête-à-tête table, a corner-lover, and, because of its pedestal base, a great space-saver.

the seventeenth century, prompted by changing social patterns, and the twentieth, prompted by new technologies. In seventeenth-century France, new concepts in privacy and comfort led to innovative French artistry devoted to rooms of individual, instead of general use—the music room, morning room, salon, boudoir, and dining room. And with these rooms also came the design of special-interest tables: the combined toilette-and-writing table, known today as the vanity-desk or lady's cabinet; the writing-fire screen that permitted letters to be written so feet were kept warm without faces being scorched; and the card table—a circular, square, tripod, pedestal, or folding beauty of wood with marquetry, inlay, or painted decoration. Other countries, following suit from the French, created small stands and tables for specific purposes: the basic stand, globe stand, urn stand, kettle stand, music or reading stand,

and plant stand. Step tables were created for "ascending high beds." Worktables ranged from baize-covered lift-lid styles with candle slides for reading and writing to highly ornamental tables with hinged tops and attached silk bags to hold sewing and needlepoint.

Coffee and cocktail tables

The introduction of tea-, coffee-, and chocolate-drinking in the middle of the seventeenth century contributed to new table styles, just as cocktails have prompted the cocktail table and snacking the snack table in the twentieth century. The butler's tray table, fairly common in the days of butlers, is the forerunner of today's coffee table in front of a sofa or love seat. It was so called because four end leaves fold up and lock, enabling the butler to remove the entire tray top, tea things and all. Tea tables with pull-out candle slides were introduced into

Three-tiered lamp table, 26 inches high, is several inches taller than generally customary to suit it to high-armed sofas. Crafted of solid cherry with shelves of maple veneers, this table could also be piled with plants.

The party-scaled table serves all meals and games, as well as homework and hobbies between times. It is finished in an impervious plastic, set on a weighted, space-saving pedestal base. Companion chairs are on small ball casters.

paign chest types, to hexagons of Spanish influence, to cabinets with doors, to lift-lid designs that store party paraphernalia inside, to lean spindle-legged one-drawer types.

Space savers

Perhaps the most ingenious of space savers, also serving as lamp or end tables, are stacks and nests of tables. Usually they are a duo of smaller and smallest tables that telescope into the largest, or "mother," table, or stack on top of each other beneath the biggest.

Multipurpose tables

Few tables throughout history were for decoration only. The possible exceptions are the console, or wall-hung, often used for sheer show; the corner table, useful for rounding off un-

Stacking tables of molded fiber glass, available in a choice of colors, serve equally well for snacks or seating.

Fold-out table with four leaves extends to 76 inches, and a center leg provides additional support. Insert two extra leaves to stretch table to maximum of 104 inches. Inside drawer stores linens; bottom shelf, extra leaves.

seventeenth-century England and, a short time later, were introduced with tea into the American colonies.

End tables

Innumerable small compact desks and cabinets for ladies evolved during the seventeenth and eighteenth centuries, among them the sewing and writing tables styled for salon or parlor use, and the sofa table, an essential to hold needlework or necessary writing materials within arm's reach.

With the advent of oil lamps, then kerosene, gas, and, ultimately, electric lamps, the end table and lamp table became major ingredients of living room decoration. Sizes and styles are innumerable, and range from pedestals to cam-

pleasant angles; and the cube, primarily a geometric measurement of space. Most tables are multipurpose, even the ones previously mentioned. Add to the obvious the less-obvious double- or triple-duty types: the curio and collector's tables, frequently surfaced with a soft fabric or topped with a hinged glass lid. Although conspicuously beautiful, they also serve to keep cherished collections within touch as well as sight. Bench tables serve not only for seating but can also hold storage stacks in a pier at one end. Bunching tables appear to be a single large-scale entity until they are separated into wedges or squares that serve for snacks or extra seating. One of the humblest dining tables, the church-born refectory, is an early example of an extension table that serves both business and pleasure. High-low tables, the latest mechanical-genius designs, raise or lower to party or dining height.

Styles and materials

Styles of tables conveniently fall into traditional, country, and contemporary or modern. These categories tend to refer more to the materials used and the room decor than to the origins of the designs. For example, a traditional decor would call for woods of intrinsic beauty such as mahogany, cherry, walnut, and teak, and styles relating to formal social habits such as a dining table with flared tripod legs, a butler's tray table, a candlestand.

Country decor calls for woods of more robust and enduring nature such as pine, oak, and maple, not only raw-figured, but often improved by painted decoration. And country styles relate to provincial or suburban informality and might include a trestle dining table, a step table, a sewing table, a plant stand.

Contemporary, or "of today," implies modern materials such as plastic, glass, and chrome, and styles tending to be angular and geometric, such as the Parsons or cube. Contemporary table styles also can be an eclectic mix of several classic styles for several purposes, each

Scaled to fit neatly beside an upholstered chair or sofa, this 23-inch-high nest of tables is artfully designed to serve several functions. The rimmed top of the largest table is big enough to hold a lamp and decorative accessories; both the smaller ones can be useful as auxiliary tables for buffet dining, for coffee or cocktails. These are of mahogany with walnut veneer.

"contemporary" in its own time. For example, a Tudor-age refectory dining table of wood, an eighteenth-century campaign chest tipped in brass, a twentieth-century Parsons table, or stacks made of plastic.

Stone is the first material known to have been shaped by man into tables or stands, by the Egyptians millennia ago. And in succeeding ancient Greek and Roman cultures, stone tables were always shaped, never constructed, because of the weight of stone. Consequently, the easy graces of lightness and mobility were unknown. Tables were unable to play an important occasional role in society until man made them out of wood, at first as simple as planks and unadorned; then so extravagantly inlaid, inset, carved, and decorated as to be works of art in themselves.

Spain's Golden Age of the early sixteenth century produced extraordinary decoration out of the rich ebony, mahogany, silver, gold, and precious stones that poured in from conquests and expeditions throughout the Orient and the New World. The most basic table of wood was embellished with metal or inlaid with stones.

Renaissance Italy, working almost invariably in walnut wood, left no table surface untreated by elaborate hand carving, gilt trim, or appliqué. France, during the Louis courts, assigned ébénistes, or carvers specializing in ebony, to the courts, and successfully imitated and often improved ancient Eastern techniques such as marquetry and lacquering. England, during the early Tudor and Jacobean days, worked in oak and, as the Empire grew, in exotic imported materials from the world over. Colonial and post-Revolutionary America, resorting to native

◄ The undulating curves of an elliptical table and companion fiddleback chairs are in the Chippendale style, introduced to the American colonies about mid-seventeenth century. The combination of antique styles, modern architecture, and sumptuous color is attractive and tasteful.

Heavy twin tables, set on massive pedestals, lend richness to an all-purpose room in combination with "floating" chests hung between walnut columns against walls covered with apricot grass cloth. The two game-size tables push together to make one long dining table.

Overscaled cocktail table in checkerboard design is a space-shaper of the 70s, lighter in weight than it looks because it is made not of wood but of molded plastic. As a result, it not only is stunning but stainproof.

designs in the twentieth century, easily manipulated by industrial process into newer, lighter, and often stronger table forms. A Parsons School of Design class exercise called for a worktable made from planks and 2x4s, and a nameless student in the class came up with a table brazenly plain, interesting, simple enough to blend harmoniously with traditional and country furniture, though sufficiently innovative to more than hold its own with modern decor. The Parsons table now is made of wood or plastic laminate and finished in lacquer or foil, fabric or tortoiseshell, or vinyl simulations of all natural materials—and can even be improvised out of pine stock and covered in wallpaper. It comes in all sizes, from dining to hall console to low, floor-hugging chairside tables reminiscent of ancient Egyptian game-table styles.

The twentieth century also made possible sculpturelike tables of free-form plate glass set upon free-form wooden bases whose parts are interchangeable at will; and tables of integrally colored plastic and fiber glass, of soft, smooth

woods, specialized in tables of maple, pine, oak, birch, and, occasionally, cherry. Mahogany, teak, and rosewood were, and still are, imported.

New designs
Except for the mid-seventeenth century of Louis XV, more emphasis was placed on table decoration than on innovative design. Two centuries passed before design again concerned itself with experimental form and relevance to function. Abetted by new technologies, designers reinterpreted metal, wood, and glass, and began experimenting in plastic. Marcel Breuer, inspired by the tubular metal handlebars of his bicycle, introduced nonresilient chrome tubing for table frames. Le Corbusier, inspired by the free-flowing lines of Thonet bentwood furniture of a century before, produced bent laminated wood

A small fabric-covered table is tailor-made for people on the move. It can be disassembled and stored flat. Construct the base out of two pieces of ¾ inch plywood, each 29 inches high and 16 inches wide. The top is two thicknesses of the ¾-inch plywood. Bottom piece of the top is X-slotted so bases lock into the slots. Apply fabric with white glue and varnish the outside surface.

finish and great strength and durability—in conventional or amorphous shapes. Folding designs of plywood with plastic tops and a simply but cleverly braced system of metal legs helped make occasional tables into aesthetic necessities.

Tables of the twentieth century, whether man- or machine-made, whether of steel, wood, plywood, plastic, other metal, are generally clean, simple, and logical, frequently interchangeable. Such designs as the cube and the Parsons owe a debt not only to United States invention but to German experimentation, Danish craftsmanship, Japanese integration of form with technology, and Italian daring with plastics.

Where will you place them?

Clearly tables are the most functional and versatile pieces of furniture in the home. And, since there are so many varieties in styles and functions, no decorating problem need go unsolved for the right choice of table, arranged to best advantage. Tables for conventional dining are the center of attention. Tables for dining in

This bunching group allows you to add, subtract, or divide individual units depending on the occasion and the space available. Triangles have polished chrome frames and are topped with smoked glass.

Designs for dining include round glass-top table with a triform chrome-plated steel base and contour-shaped caneback chairs with chrome-plated steel frames, black vinyl upholstered seats, and rosewood-trimmed armrests.

"Ls" or alcoves can hug a wall, drop-leaf style, or angle out from a wall perpendicularly, or can be one of the types that drifts down out of a modular wall cabinet.

Occasional tables can have fixed positions where they are most useful, although they need not remain there indefinitely. Desk-tables should be oriented to the most appropriate lighting; planters with real plants to the best light and ventilation. Little seat- or bench-tables, such as hassocks on wheels, can be pushed out of the way of busy traffic patterns. Coffee and cocktail tables are usually companions to major seating, either positioned in front of or between sofas and chairs.

Stacks and nests fortunately fit anywhere, often at chairside or sofaside. More permanent card and game tables can be a focal point of a room or double as brunch tables in large bed-

rooms. Folding tables of all kinds have the ability to store in closets. Multipurpose tables almost determine their own positions in a room: the bench table with storage deck usually remains against a wall, although it can be equally effective as a room divider. Collector's or curio tables demand to be within arm's reach of leisure seating. Certain classic table styles, such as Parsons, in varying sizes, colors, and textures can go virtually anywhere and serve nearly every need.

The prime advantage of a table is that it can serve you both functionally and aesthetically. The best of table design offers both; additionally, a table, given proper placement, should be a means to save space and steps.

An interesting aspect of tables is that they tempt the ablest as well as the most amateurish do-it-yourselfer to make them. It is possible to make Parsons styles from four solid square legs, topped by a frame of 2x4s, topped by a plank of wood. One can make tables of acrylic plastic using straight sheeting or rods, or bend it by heating to create more ornate forms. Even the trickiest built-ins are possible with right materials, good directions, and patience.

◄ Or try a patio table of decorative concrete blocks. As pictured here, each leg is just two concrete blocks mortared together. The wood top is made of select cedar 1x2s that need no finishing. The top boards, nailed to 1x4 braces underneath, simply sit on the blocks; plan the wood parts to be heavy enough to stay in place. Or nail 2x2 cleats to the bottom of the tabletop to fit over blocks. You can build benches and smaller tables just as easily.

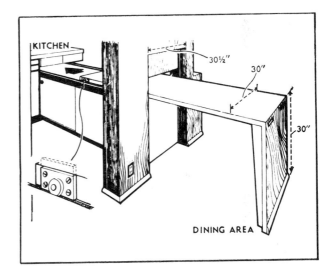

The ingenious multipurpose table here is a combination sliding counter for kitchen work-top space; a dining room table, a buffet or beverage-serving surface; a surface for snacks, desk work, or games. It is both good-looking and practical as a built-in or pullout. The table is 6½ feet long, will extend far enough to seat three on each side. And it can include a permanent counter below the pullout for extra kitchen work space when the table is in use. Use steel ball-bearing wardrobe closet rollers; the diagram shows how to mount the hardware upside down so wheels roll on scored track of the lower counter. Cut off portion of metal plate that extends beyond table thickness. The slide-up door above the table is held in place with a turnbuckle. A shelf simplifies installation and forms an attractive shadow box, too. A wall outlet or an electrical plug-in strip accommodates small electric appliances.

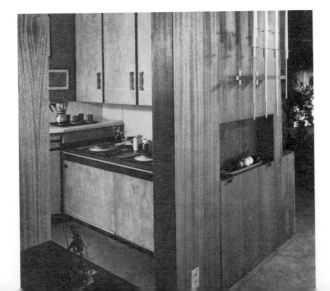

How to Achieve Perfection
For Your Entertaining Table

If you are the best cook in town, guests will gratefully, even joyfully, eat in the kitchen off paper plates laid on oilcloth. But a good cook deserves a proper setting to display her gifts, as a guest deserves a festive welcome and your family deserves a table that is appealing to the eye as well as to the appetite.

Haute cuisine places almost as much importance on the aesthetic presentation of food as it does on its taste. Certainly restaurants recognize the commercial value of atmosphere, planning their decor with as much care as their menus. Most housewives cannot, of course, compete with a master chef, and it would be unseemly to imitate the theatricality of a large restaurant. On a domestic scale, however, dramatic effects can be achieved with simple means and a little daring.

The following discussion offers pointers on selecting and assembling the elements of an attractive table setting—china, crystal, silver, and linen—as well as a discussion of basic design tools—color, style, and pattern.

Choosing the style to set

Table appointments have a style just as your furniture does. Decorating styles, in effect, establish the theme for dining fashions.

For the sake of simplicity, table appointments can be categorized in three great styles: classic, country, and contemporary. If your dining area is separated from the rest of the house, the table appointments may be a complete departure from decorating themes in other rooms. If the dining area is not a separate room, on the other hand, the table appointments should be in keeping with the surrounding decor. Most homemakers find that the table appointments inspired by their favorite furniture periods are personally most pleasing. As with many generalizations, however, these are open to wide variations.

Modern casual flatware and dinnerware can be stunning in an Early American dining room or kitchenette. It is unlikely, though, that a complete disregard of design inspiration will be very successful. The same contemporary ware might very well be a disaster in a formal dining room.

Classic table settings

Classifying your dining room furniture is the first step in coordinating your dinnerware. Perhaps it would be best accessorized with classic table appointments. These are all characterized by a certain formality and by ornamental detail inspired by ancient sources such as early Greece.

Typical of the classic in tableware are plates with scrolled rims or borders and patterns including wreaths, scrolls, and allover floral designs. Glassware, almost invariably stemware, is characterized by a pure and simple silhouette but is often elaborately ornamented with cut or etched patterns and with gold or silver edging. Flatware may be simple in form, like the eighteenth-century fiddleback pattern, or richly decorated with scrolls and flowers, following baroque design.

Whether formal or romantic in mood, classic table appointments reflect Old World grace and luxury.

A harmonious use of simple flowers in yellow and white for a symmetrical table setting in the eighteenth-century tradition is a perfect example of balance in shape, form, and color. Texture is considered, too, in the gleaming surface of the table, heavily cut crystal goblets, and crystal turkeys on either side of the centerpiece.

Country table settings

The term "country" covers a range of currently popular styles from Early American to Spanish and even Mexican. All have the same basic characteristics, emphasizing color, weight, and pattern. Heavy pottery, semiporcelain, and ironstone with geometric and floral patterns fall into this category.

Glassware is heavy, often colored, and goblets are short-stemmed. Early American milk glass fits well into this style. Pewter and copper holloware, even brass accessories, are associated with country styles. Country flatware is semiornate and also includes reproductions of antique patterns.

Texture typifies country table linens, which frequently have rough, interesting weaves. Plaids and floral prints are especially suitable. Handcrafted objects fit beautifully with country table appointments. The woman who has developed a craft talent, whether for ceramics or for needlework, will find that she can make handsome and original table appointments to accent country pieces.

Contemporary table settings

The third basic style, contemporary, is for those who prefer a clean and uncluttered look. Bold colors and bright accents characterize this style. Dramatic impact is the intended effect.

Contemporary table settings can be either formal or informal in feeling. Contemporary dinnerware designs are clean-cut, with accent on form and color. Often its glaze is crackled or crazed to add textural interest. The current

explosion of exciting modern home furnishings has stimulated a matching explosion in contemporary dinnerware designs at all price ranges. Designs are usually overscaled and boldly colored, and are sometimes deeply cut or carved on the surface.

Contemporary linens are colorful, often printed, and of a wide variety of materials, such as cotton broadcloth and synthetic fabrics—even wet-look vinyls and metallic weaves. They are often wash-and-wear or permanent-press fabrics.

Tableware designers today adapt traditional designs to meet current tastes and needs. Often, this allows for the combining of styles into effective and highly individual settings. This mixture of the best elements of traditional design and modern taste is called the eclectic style. Since many homes are furnished eclectically, many people will want to combine elements of more than one style in their table settings. Choose your dinnerware and other table appointments with an eye to effective mixing and

Dinnerware supplied all the hints for this coordinated place setting. Its celadon green suggested the matching napkin, and the terra-cotta cup suggested the striped place mat and amber tumbler. The daisy bouquet is almost inevitable, but a single zinnia adds a graceful note.

◀ Country means colorful in this audacious table setting. Mexican tinware plates are trimmed with bits of colored tile and tiny mirrors. The distinctive tablecloth is an Indian print that was intended as a bedspread.

matching of tableware and accessories. This gives variety to daily settings as well as stretching service for large gatherings.

Flatware

The most important choice in table appointments is flatware, partly because of its permanence, partly because of its relative costliness. Since it is practically indestructible, there is no reason why you cannot use even sterling silver flatware for everyday family dining. Generally speaking, the least expensive flatware is stainless steel, while silver or gold electroplated flatware is somewhere between sterling silver and stainless steel. Vermeil—sterling silver with a gold overlay—is considered the choicest flatware and is, expectedly, the most expensive.

Any flatware marked "sterling" must meet the standard silver-copper proportion for sterling made into law by King Edward I of England. The ratio is 92½ parts silver to 7½ parts copper. The copper is added to give strength to this basically malleable metal.

Silver-plated flatware is made from a base metal plus layers of silver plating. In better qualities, extra silver has been added at points of greatest wear, such as spoon backs, and it carries a life-long guarantee.

Stainless steel is extremely popular because it is durable and economical and does not tarnish. Recently, matching patterns in silver and stainless steel have been introduced.

In all three main types of flatware, different qualities are available. Quality factors include balance, both in the hand and to the eye. Lines should be graceful, with good proportion of handles to working parts.

Many sterling patterns and some stainless steel and silver plate patterns are guaranteed to be in open stock for years. This is an important factor when an entire set cannot be purchased at once. If possible, however, try to buy complete services, as this can result in substantial savings. Sterling silver is sold by the individual piece, in place settings, and in sets. Stainless steel and silver plate are available in place settings but are most often purchased in standard services for eight or twelve. When you buy a set of flatware, basic serving pieces are usually included. To determine the number of place settings needed, go by the size of the family plus the extras needed for guests. If buffet entertaining is your basic party style, extra teaspoons and forks may be a more practical purchase than extra place settings. In any case, serving pieces should be included in your flatware inventory. These can match your basic set, although special-purpose pieces like cake servers may be of a different pattern. For dessert service, contrasting pieces—antique silver or gold-electroplated forks and spoons—are especially effective.

Flatware patterns in all materials usually fall into the three basic table styles. For further information, see *Flatware,* Vol. 8, p. 1414.

Dinnerware

Most women want at least two sets of dishes, one for every day that is casual and not too costly, and a set of fine china for special occasions. Of the latter, six place settings is about the minimum for entertaining.

Five-piece place settings are the most common. These include a dinner plate, dessert or salad plate, a butter plate, a cup, and a saucer. Basic serving pieces, such as vegetable bowls and platters, are a necessity in china or metal.

Everyday dinnerware is often sold in services for four or eight, usually with basic serving pieces included. Since you will see and handle it every day, it is important that it be pleasing to both sight and touch. Many women are more adventurous with their everyday dinnerware choices than with their fine china, since normal breakage will require eventual replacement. The variety of patterns and prices available in casual dinnerware makes such planning practical. Many of the less-expensive everyday sets are not guaranteed to be in open stock, should you want to replace only part.

In this country table setting, the chunky form of modern sterling silver is decorated with a motif strikingly similar to that on the pottery dinnerware. A whimsical centerpiece features unusual bouquets made of bright buttons.

Suitability to your needs should govern both fine and casual china choices. If casual entertaining is your forte, check some of the new casual patterns designed expressly for entertaining, with features like extra-large plates.

Dinnerware should coordinate with your flatware, and then set the tone for the rest of the table. The color and pattern on the plates is the single most important factor in choosing linens, glassware, and even the centerpiece flowers.

Classic dinnerware patterns are rich in detail and intricate design. Traditional motifs include reeds, ribbons, horns of plenty, medallions,

The handsome but neutral china pattern shown in these two pictures adapts itself with distinction to two very different table settings. Combined with stark black-and-white goblets and black-and-gold napkins, the precise lines of its trim provide a delicate but emphatic counterpoint to a contemporary setting. Combined with red earthenware and heavy traditional silver, the same pattern offers an unassertive background for a bright country setting.

scrolls, scenic patterns, and allover floral designs delicately worked, or the classic old country rose. The decoration is dignified, symmetrical, and subdued, in contrast to the bolder, more casual colors and patterns of contemporary or country dinnerware. Often, classic dinnerware is decorated with either gold or platinum and has a high glaze.

Country dinnerware often has raised or grooved designs. The glazes vary from smooth to matte and rough, and the colors are often either earthy clay tones or bright as garden flowers. It may be decorated with stylized flowers or geometric figures painted in a rustic style.

Contemporary dinnerware takes its character primarily from clean-lined forms. Both fine bone china and inexpensive casual dinnerware often have no applied ornamentation, but may be decorated with starkly contemporary motifs. Glazes and colors will also vary in this style.

Glassware

Colored or clear, fragile or massive, glassware offers the finishing touch to your table setting. Beautiful formal china demands equally elegant crystal in a compatible design, and sturdy country earthenware calls for correspondingly heavy glass tumblers.

A basic table service of crystal would include stemware—water goblets, sherbet glasses, possibly all-purpose wine glasses—as well as 7- or 8-inch liner plates that can double as dessert plates. You might want to supplement these basics with glasses for iced tea, champagne, or parfaits.

Crystal is more durable than it looks and, with ordinary precautions against breakage, can last for years. However, it is a good idea to make sure that the pattern you choose is available in open stock for replacements.

The quality of crystal can be judged by its clarity and brilliance and by the telltale resonance it manifests when struck with a fingernail. Also test glassware for balance and comfort in the hand.

Fine stemware is often decorated with either etchings or cuttings, and may have gold or platinum bands. Decorative motifs are sometimes identical to that of coordinated china.

Casual glassware can also be handcrafted and elegant. Often colored, casual glassware can be hand-blown or pressed, a method of pressing molten glass either by hand or machine, or a combination of both, into a mold. The heavy weight of pressed glass suits it to use with country, and in some cases contemporary, table settings.

Everyday glassware can be anything from plastic to pressed glass. Make sure that it is comfortable for both man-sized hands and little fingers. The sizes most often wanted for everyday use are water tumblers and juice glasses. These can do double duty as tall and short bar glasses.

Colored glassware makes an exceptionally handsome appearance on the table, but in use it may have rather unpleasant psychological effects—imagine, say, chocolate milk in a dark blue glass. Wines and liquors should always be served in clear glasses except in the case of German white wines, which are traditionally (but not necessarily) served in pale green glasses. See *Glassware,* Vol. 10, p. 1756.

Pressed milk glass is a classic country American glassware. A charming Valentine's Day dessert setting makes full use of the gleaming white traditionally beaded glass by coupling it with red tablecloth and carnations.

◄Monochromatic scheme, inspired by springtime pinks of early peonies and apple blossoms, provides a choice setting for delicately fluted china—itself trimmed with dainty pink flowers —and traditional silver. A circular tablecloth, although it will require piecing, can be made by any competent seamstress.

Pale mauve place mats reinforce the color of the marble-ized salad plates in this setting clearly designed for a ladies' luncheon. Purple and yellow pansies—and the pink sashes on the porcelain musicians—consolidate the color scheme, while the milky translucence of the short-stemmed goblets provides a cool and delicate accent.

Linens

Measure your table before you begin to shop for linens. Remember to include the table leaves in your figuring if you usually use the table extended. The exact length and width are very important in selecting the right cloth. So that the hem of the tablecloth will drop gracefully on all sides of the table, allow a 16- to 24-inch margin on all sides. Never buy a tablecloth that has less than 10 inches of fabric to hang over the edges; it will look skimpy.

Check the fiber content on linens. This can make a difference in both price and durability as well as in the amount of work entailed in laundering. The price of linens also depends on the amount of finishing done by hand—whether the pieces are decorated with hemstitching or fagoting, whether appliqués or embroidery are hand-stitched or machine-stitched, whether the hem was turned by hand or by machine or not at all.

Classic table appointments are often displayed on damask cloths. Considered the aristocrat of fine table coverings, damask is a cloth with a very fine, intricate weave that produces a flat textured pattern with a permanent luster. Damasks may be made of cotton, linen, or rayon, or in combinations of these fibers.

Lace cloths and fine linen weaves, either appliquéd or plain, are also used for classic table settings. Usually, napkins match or harmonize in a classic table setting. White and ecru are traditional colors. Both show off the beauty or pattern of fine china and crystal.

Both contemporary and country tables offer great scope to the woman who can manipulate color, pattern, and texture with imagination and assurance.

The more simplified patterns and naturalistic homespun textures provide a congenial background for country tables. If pattern is a strong element in your table appointments, a beautiful solid linen cloth may be the best accessory. Contrasting napkins individualize place settings.

There are, in fact, no rules governing the choices of linens for informal table settings. The wide range of exciting prints and sumptuous textures available at reasonable cost allows you to vary the mood of your table settings without substituting tableware.

Most fine tablecloths will require special laundering care, but in shopping for casual linens take advantage of wash-and-wear fabrics.

Place mats, because they are easy to care for and relatively inexpensive, are practical linens, or more often plastics, for everyday use. Their utility need not be limited to family meals, however. Fine embroidered-linen place mats provide an elegant background for a classic luncheon table setting, while bright prints and

For the woman who enjoys handicrafts, table settings offer a practical outlet for creative energies. This green-and- yellow place mat with matching napkin clip was made of plastic pellets baked in the oven on a cookie sheet.

textured weaves—even shiny vinyl—offer a fresh approach to informal dinner settings.

Ready-made place mats generally range in size from 12 to 14 inches deep and from 16 to 18 inches wide. Size should be chosen according to the proportions of your table and the number of diners it will accommodate; overlarge mats will make the tabletop appear cramped while undersized mats will look skimpy. Place mats must, of course, be ample enough to prevent crowding of plates and flatware.

Place mats are also available in a variety of shapes. As a rule, rectangular mats are best suited to square or rectangular tables, although oval mats afford a pleasant change of pace. Place mats with curved hems look best on round tables. Wedge-shaped mats, with the outer edge conforming to the arc of the table's edge, give a custom-designed look to a table setting.

Table runners should be approximately a foot wide and may fit the length of the table exactly or have a drop at each end of from 8 to 10 inches. You can use a center runner that holds

one place setting at each end of the table with mats along the sides. Equally effective, if less expected, is the placement of a pair of runners stretched parallel along the edges of the table.

Ready-made runners are not as widely available, and certainly not in such variety, as tablecloths and place mats. To make one yourself, however, is an easy task involving only hemming.

Matching napkins are often sold with tablecloths in sets of four, six, eight, or twelve, depending on the size of the tablecloth. Napkins are usually cut square and range in size from the luxurious dinner napkin, 22 or 24 inches square, through the luncheon napkin, around 17 inches square, to the dainty tea napkin, about a foot square.

Almost any material will serve to make attractive napkins, from traditional damask to gaudy printed linen or cotton. Fabric texture should, however, be lintless and fairly crisp in the hand, and its surface should not be too smooth—satin, for example, is unsuitable. Nor should the weave be too coarse or nubby.

Although convention calls for pale colors with traditional table furnishings, a bold color may be appropriate as well as exciting. Here, pale green grapes spill from a straw cornucopia onto a brilliant heliotrope tablecloth—a daring color scheme that is nonetheless firmly related to the flowered china and amethyst crystal.

Two china patterns, different in form but similar in coloring, were specially chosen for their capacity to mix well and to bring out the best in each other. The autumnal earth colors of the dinnerware are repeated in the plaid tablecloth and a centerpiece of gourds and mums.

Side runners isolate these multiple centerpieces while unifying the place settings. Bold-patterned china is well suited to the bold-patterned runners. Bouquets of red berries and English ivy march straight down the center of the table, their colors vivid against wood.

Color—a basic ingredient

A variation of color on your table can alter the appearance of the entire dining room, and offers an easy and inexpensive way to celebrate an occasion or simply to mark a change of season. Possibilities for color schemes are limited only by fixed elements (china, glasses, and the room's basic color scheme), somewhat by the style of your table furnishings, by your budget, and by your own inventiveness.

You may want to have a fairly conventional color scheme for everyday purposes: bright reds or blues or perhaps soothing pastels. An adventurous orange-and-magenta-print tablecloth that would be exhilarating once a year may quickly become tiresome if seen once a day.

If the style of your table furnishings is classic, you will probably want linens of quiet colors—

Sea green and mariner's blue combine in an ideal table setting for a boating party—or for a land-based picnic. A bright yellow napkin and an unexpected bouquet of red radishes provide warm accents for the cool color scheme.

white, ecru, or, perhaps, for an informal occasion, delicate pastels—to display the rich ornament of silver and crystal. There are, however, no limitations on the quality and quantity of color you can add with flowers and candles. These appurtenances, temporary by nature, provide elementary tools for table decorations.

Although one ordinarily thinks of a restricted and formal arrangement of pale colors in relation to classic settings—opulent peonies and pink roses, perhaps, flanked by tall white candles— you need not limit yourself so strictly. No flower, however lowly, is ever inappropriate as long as the overall scale of the arrangement is suitable to the size of the table and the proportions of its furnishings. A centerpiece of boisterous marigolds or a small bouquet of wild daisies and buttercups at each place setting would be both becoming to a classically appointed table.

As with classic, so with formal contemporary table settings, which seem to call for a certain restraint in the use of color. If your contemporary tableware is white, a dark blue or green tablecloth will reveal the silhouettes of plates and crystal. Brilliant prints should be avoided: they will obscure the refinement of line that characterizes modern design.

Country and informal contemporary table settings, however, almost demand an exuberant and unconventional approach to color. Pastels, if selected with imaginative discrimination, can be refreshing and even daring—apricot and bright yellow, or Nile green and pink. Informal settings are also hospitable to strong colors.

Vary your table decorations according to the season. For an autumn table setting, use warm earth colors—terra-cotta, gold, and rich brown, accompanied by brilliant fall leaves and bronze-colored chrysanthemums. In warm weather, use clear blues and fresh greens, and whatever flowers, wild or garden-grown, that are in season.

Luxurious and vivid colors brighten wintertime table settings—lush teal blue, a sumptuous maroon, or an uncompromising red. Although hothouses provide flowers year-round, the sea-

A contemporary table setting is usually stark, dramatic, but also inviting, as in this striking black-and-white scheme. A pair of mushroom-shaped candy jars provides a background for one stunning touch of geranium red.

Despite employing no fewer than three colors and two china patterns, this table setting displays uncommon subtlety of color relationships. Pastel shades are picked up and intensified by the jewel tones of tumblers and compotes.

sonal absence of homegrown flowers offers an opportunity to create nonfloral centerpieces from evergreen branches and pinecones, or fruits, or bittersweet and dried grasses.

A setting for a buffet dinner, where initial visual impact is more important than a relaxing atmosphere, affords still another opportunity for daring table decorations. Forceful color combinations that would be too strong for a quiet dinner—such as Halloween black and orange—are quite appropriate at a buffet.

For further ideas on colors and table decorations, see *Candles,* Vol. 4, p. 690; *Centerpieces,* Vol. 4, p. 730; *Color,* Vol. 5, p. 842; *Flower Arranging,* Vol. 8, p. 1442; and *Party Ideas,* Vol. 14, p. 2499.

Serving with style

The rules of etiquette for table settings are determined by common sense and consideration for your guests' convenience.

Formal dinners, apart from catered banquets, are a comparative rarity in these servantless

days. Some authorities on etiquette, in fact, say that servantless formal service is a contradiction. Nonetheless, there are degrees of informality.

A formal dinner, or any important dinner, calls for a full tablecloth, flowers, and candles. In any table setting, you should allow a width of 20 to 30 inches for each place setting. All appointments are placed about one inch from the

◄ Only in the strict sense of the word is this startling black-and-white table setting "colorless." The unorthodox black napkin and the frosted goblet stand out in a glittering combination of crystal, mirror, and silver.

If you are at a loss for a centerpiece idea, take a cue from your linens. A mass of roses and a brilliant print tablecloth seem almost to be colorful reflections of one another on this forceful but feminine tea table.

edge of the table, forks to the left of the center, knives and spoons to the right. The exception to this rule is the shrimp-cocktail fork, which is set on the right side of the plate.

Flatware is arranged in order of use from the outside. Thus you might have, on the left side of the cover, a dinner fork on the outside, a salad fork inside (if salad is served after the main course), and on the right, reading from outside to inside, a soup spoon and a dinner knife. The carving set, if it is needed, should be placed at the host's right hand.

A fresh cover is usually provided for dessert, with a dessert fork at the left or a dessert spoon at the right, or both, and a teaspoon at the far right. The dessert fork may be placed on plate.

The napkin, folded vertically, customarily lies at the left of the forks. If the setting includes a salad plate, however, the napkin must be placed in the center of the cover.

The water goblet should be placed just above the tip of the knife, with the wine goblet set diagonally to the right, roughly at the tip of the spoon.

The bread-and-butter plate goes above the forks, with the butter spreader straight across the top, and the salad plate goes to the left of the forks. Either of these plates may be omitted— butter plates, indeed, are not provided at all in very formal table settings.

Plan the order of seating before the party. Traditionally, host and hostess sit at each end of the table. The female guest of honor sits on the host's right, the male guest of honor on the hostess' right. Men and women are usually alternated around the table.

If the host serves the entire meal, plates should be stacked in front of him. He first serves the

A pattern of nosegays and streamers provided the inspiration for this table setting. The crisply executed design of the table runners is carried through in the centerpiece: milk glass containers holding daisies and ivy.

Festive Napkin Folds

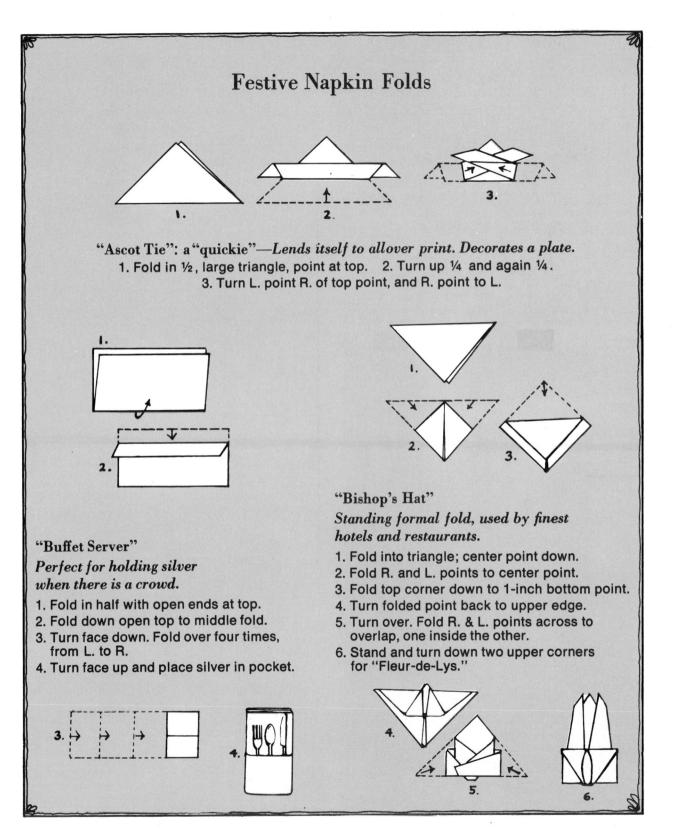

"Ascot Tie": a "quickie"—*Lends itself to allover print. Decorates a plate.*
1. Fold in ½, large triangle, point at top.   2. Turn up ¼ and again ¼.
3. Turn L. point R. of top point, and R. point to L.

"Buffet Server"
*Perfect for holding silver
when there is a crowd.*

1. Fold in half with open ends at top.
2. Fold down open top to middle fold.
3. Turn face down. Fold over four times,
   from L. to R.
4. Turn face up and place silver in pocket.

"Bishop's Hat"
*Standing formal fold, used by finest
hotels and restaurants.*

1. Fold into triangle; center point down.
2. Fold R. and L. points to center point.
3. Fold top corner down to 1-inch bottom point.
4. Turn folded point back to upper edge.
5. Turn over. Fold R. & L. points across to
   overlap, one inside the other.
6. Stand and turn down two upper corners
   for "Fleur-de-Lys."

guest of honor on his right, then the hostess, and then proceeds to serve in order from the farthest guest to the nearest, first on his right, then on his left. If the hostess serves the side dishes, she takes the second-to-last plate herself, giving the last one to the host.

In informal dining, the host customarily serves the meat if it requires carving. Otherwise, guests help themselves from serving dishes passed counterclockwise from the host's right. For the sake of safety, unwieldy dishes—a platter of corn on the cob, for instance—should not be passed.

This bridal luncheon setting features rose-patterned china and a beribboned nosegay of roses in a crystal glass. The tablecloth is of tulle, napkins are a pale rosebud pink.

Buffet settings

Although the chief charm of the buffet is its informality, this style of dining can be just as elegant as any formal meal. Providing the food is attractively served and the decorations handsome, it is the most gracious way to entertain a large number of guests.

Another of the buffet dinner's great charms is that it necessitates less last-minute work for the hostess. It does, however, require careful earlier preparation. To begin with, the menu should be planned so that all foods can be eaten without a knife.

The most satisfactory plan for serving a buffet dinner is to place the table in the center of the room so that guests may circle it; for a very large group, you may want to duplicate the layout to allow for two lines of guests. If the table must be set against a wall, there should be room enough between wall and table to allow you access for replenishing the table.

Guests should first pick up their dinner plates and take a serving of the main course; both are placed at the end of the table. Other foods, such as vegetables, rolls, and relishes, go along the table. If any dishes, such as tossed salad, require two hands for serving, leave enough room on the table for guests to set their plates down. Because a diner will need one hand to hold his plate and the other to serve himself, leave flatware and napkins till last.

Beverages should be served from a sideboard or tea cart. Otherwise, leave them on the table to be picked up after silverware and napkins.

Any "rules" of correct table setting can be broken if need be. They are, after all, devised primarily to ensure sensible organization and smooth service—and to relieve the hostess of flustering indecision.

An unusual centerpiece of twin topiaries featuring ivy, ▶ camellia leaves, and gladiola florets adds warm color and interest to this mid-winter table. Vermeil flatware and colored glasses are special notes of elegance.

The Right Type and Size for You, And Where to Place It

There is little doubt that television has changed our lives in many ways. As a source of information, education, and entertainment it has developed from a scientific and technological curiosity; as a medium of communication its role is now as important in modern life as that of the telephone and the radio.

Selection of the right television set for home use should be given the same careful consideration as the selection of any other important piece of furniture or equipment. A brief survey of your family's needs and the answers to a few questions will help you to start thinking in the right direction.

Choosing your TV set

The best way to begin is to decide first of all on how much you plan to spend for your television set. The price you can afford will be an important factor in the size and type of TV you finally choose.

Next, think about who will be using this television set most often. Will it be the only TV in your home, or will it be an additional one? If this is to be the family television set and the only one in the home, then you should consider a TV with a reasonably large screen that can be viewed by groups of four or more people together. The smaller screens are best for individual use or for viewing by two or three people in a relatively small area.

Television screens are measured diagonally and can range in size from 6 to 24 inches. Screens that measure between 18 and 24 inches are large enough for group viewing in a living room. Sets that are between 12 and 18 inches are suitable for a smaller area like a den or bedroom. The smallest TV screens, those that are between 6 and 12 inches, are ideally suited for very small areas and individual viewing, such as on a desktop or kitchen counter.

In the early days of television it was not unusual to walk into a room and be confronted with the blank staring eye of the TV screen, which was a novelty and therefore the center of attraction. It was as much a distraction when it was turned off as it was an attraction when it was turned on. New developments in set design and the creativity of furniture and interior designers have changed all that. Now you can include television in your decorating plans attractively and inconspicuously.

Consoles

For use in a living room, consider a television set that is enclosed in a handsomely styled and beautifully executed piece of furniture. There is a wide variety of console television sets available today in designs and finishes to blend attractively with almost any furniture or decorating scheme. And, because of new engineering techniques, the TV sets themselves are, slimmer and sleeker in construction. You can now find consoles designed to fit into almost any size area. Many of them come with decorative doors to conceal the screen or open flat when the set is in use.

When you contemplate buying a console TV, it is important to remember that you are really making a dual purchase. The television set should be of the size and type that will best serve your family's needs. It should also be of sturdy construction and placed in the cabinet in such a way as to be accessible for repairs. The con-

Here is an elegant three-section wall unit that separates living and dining areas. Plan your own units so they touch the ceiling or, as shown here, a beam. This unit is only 19 inches deep, but contains an entire entertainment center for the living room. Music components are on a convenient level, with speakers at the upper corners. The television cubicle, which has its own matching double-hinged door, is flanked on either side by generous tape-and record-storage cabinets. The sections of this wall unit are all separate but joined by the wide black trim boards. This device makes it much simpler to build, and much easier to move or change at some later date.

sole itself should be of the quality and design that is most compatible with your other furnishings. It is not necessary, however, to try to find a console in a style and finish that will exactly match the pieces in your room. Many styles and finishes are complementary to each other and provide interesting contrast in a decorating plan.

In addition to serving as an enclosure for your television set, a console can provide a focal point for your room arrangement. And if you select one with extra cabinets it will add valuable space that can be used for such things as hard-to-store serving trays, table linens, or bar glasses and accessories.

Table models

Large table-model television sets lend themselves to a variety of decorating ideas for convenient family viewing. Standing on a table with easy-rolling casters, for example, the table-model TV can be placed unobtrusively in the living room or family room and pulled forward for comfortable viewing by all. With an extra-long cord it can even be pulled into the dining room for watching special events.

This type of set also fits extremely well into plans that call for a built-in TV. A pleasing and convenient arrangement can be built for a home entertainment center that can also include your hi-fi equipment and your radio. Plan the placement of components and speakers so that your television is located where it can be viewed without obstruction but will not be the center of attraction. For added flexibility in this kind of arrangement, you can mount the television set on a turntable so that it can be seen from any part of the room. When planning a built-in arrangement for your television, be sure to allow sufficient space around it for adequate circulation of air. In addition, the controls on this and all types of TV sets should be easy to reach but not so obvious as to detract from the appearance of the set.

Portables

While table-model television sets offer more flexibility than the console models in room planning, those that are classified as portable provide even more mobility and versatility of use. A lightweight portable with a convenient carrying handle can travel readily from the bedroom to the kitchen, to the laundry, to the patio. The case should be well built to withstand this kind of use, and the handle should be inconspicuous though comfortable for its purpose.

How important is this kind of mobility to the needs of your family? If conserving space is more important to you than the ability of your TV to travel, a portable may still be the right kind of television set for you. Usually compact in styling and light in weight, a portable TV is well suited to the kind of situation where a bulkier and heavier model would be impractical. A shelf in the book-lined reading area of the den or living room is a good location for a portable television set since it requires a minimum of space. Another convenient place for a versatile portable TV is on a shelf over the handyman's workbench.

Having decided upon the most suitable kind of television set for your family's needs, it is now important to select the best location to provide maximum convenience and comfortable viewing. An extremely effective way to incor-

A fireplace is a natural focal point for a living room. In this comfortable setting, the wood storage box in the fireplace opening houses a television set instead of firewood. For protection against the heat of the fireplace, a 2- or 3-inch fiber glass insulation bat and a ¾-inch plywood panel should be added to the side of the woodbox. As an extra safety precaution, check with your TV serviceman to be sure there is sufficient air circulation around the set. Ask him to check also to be sure the set is accessible for repairs.

This family room has a warm and inviting atmosphere that ▶ makes it a natural center for informal gatherings and for family hobbies, games, and study. The built-in unit on the fireplace wall has a good-size cabinet on the bottom, shelves for books, and space for a television set with a screen that is ample for viewing in this room. The seating arrangement here is flexible since the cozy chairs by the fireplace can be easily moved on the uncarpeted floor for a better view of the TV screen. The comfortable dining chairs can provide extra seating.

A handsome wall unit can provide an expanse of shelves for the family library, a well-planned entertainment center, and valuable extra storage space. The television set, which is centered in the bottom row of cabinets, is well located for unobstructed viewing anywhere in the room. A unit of this type is usually custom-made, and consequently can be designed in a variety of styles.

porate a television set into your decorating scheme is to include it as part of a wall unit. There are a number of ways to develop the kind of unit that will best suit your family's style of living.

Create your own wall unit

A wall unit in a den or family room can serve as a convenient and attractive reading-listening-hobby center. Try combining open shelves for books and magazines with space for hi-fi, radio, and television. Create cabinets with decorative doors for the storage of records or tapes and family board games, and use a matching door front or a drop-leaf desk arrangement for the stamp or coin collector. Conceal the television set when it is not in use behind a door that matches those used on the storage cabinets and desk front.

If your TV set looks "old hat" but still works, why hide it away in a corner? You can give it a face-lifting and turn it into a good-looking new piece of furniture. To make a handsome new case like this one, build a big cube from walnut plywood. Put doors on the front, and make your TV mobile by adding a set of carpet casters. When you are not television watching, close the doors and roll the set out of the way. Write for Project Plan 3707-16.

Before and after photographs show how this bedroom wall ▶ was transformed from a bland nonentity to a glamorous and useful part of the room. Before, the wall, marred by a radiator and chopped up by three windows, was an unattractive necessity, below. The owners made do with makeshift shelving. After, right, the creation of a floor to-ceiling storage unit between windows made use of wasted space. A wide shelf at the bottom of the unit holds television set and serves as a desk. Cabinets beneath the shelf conceal the radiator and provide storage. Bright striped curtains above the shelves and at the windows unify the wall visually and give the room interest.

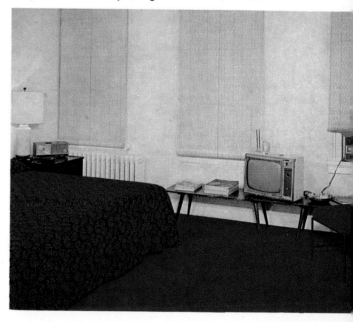

A dining room that doubles its usefulness by being a family room, too, can be as attractive as it is functional. This well-designed storage wall is made of rough-cut redwood plywood; the shelves are adjustable and each drawer is saw-marked to look like two. Here is handy storage space for games, books, and all the other family-room clutter. Notice that the television set fits neatly into its own compartment. The dining chairs, like the room itself, have little chance to stand idle most of the day since they are used for TV viewing as well.

In this elegant brown-and-white kitchen you can plan and create delicacies fit for a king. And while you are at it, the compact television set on your kitchen counter will keep you posted on the important happenings in the rest of the world. This portable TV with its darkened screen is handy enough to carry with you to a backyard barbecue, a picnic at the beach, or even on a family vacation camping trip. The handle on the top is neat in appearance, of good size for convenient carrying; and the rabbit ears fold down compactly when they are not in use.

An easy-to-create storage wall for a child's room has space for his TV set as well. Build a series of plywood boxes, all the same size, from ¾-inch plywood with ¼-inch plywood backs. Put doors on some of them and leave some of them open in front. Face two boxes with chalkboard, but be sure they are at the right height for your young artist. Stack the boxes or hang them in the pattern that best suits your needs. Leave room to slide a television set into its own space after viewing is over.

As a divider between your living room and dining area, a wall unit can add precious storage space as well as visual interest to both. In the living room, allocate some of the shelf space for books and place the TV on a low shelf. Use the space behind the television set for a cabinet that opens into the dining area. This cabinet is well situated for storing the chest that holds your flatware, or it can be fitted with one or two felt-lined and partitioned drawers to be used instead of the chest. (Either way, such a cabinet is a great convenience for table setting and serving.) Use another cabinet in the dining area, with its door hinged at the bottom so it can be used as a serving area, for liquor and bar accessories. To prevent your wall unit from appearing overpoweringly heavy, leave two or three of the shelves open to both sides. Such space is perfect for displaying a few of your family treasures: a favorite teapot, an interesting figurine, or a few large and colorful shells collected at the beach.

This bookcase-television-stereo wall unit looks like a built-in unit, but looks can fool you. It is made of ¾-inch plywood stained brown and construction tile painted black, and can be knocked down to be moved whenever the occasion arises. The bottom shelf of the unit is raised so that the television set resting on it is at a good height for viewing in this living room. Space has been left behind the shelves above the TV so that the rabbit ears can be extended for improved reception. The use of plants and flowers adds a delightful contrast to the books and stereo equipment arranged on the other shelves.

One of the many convenient ways to bring television into the bedroom is to make room for it on the shelf of a storage wall. The stacked furniture in this master bedroom combines chest space, a desk, bookshelves, and cabinets in addition to a radio and the portable TV set. The set is compact and so it can be accommodated in a rather small space. Its location is good for viewing while in bed; by simply turning the TV on its shelf it can also be seen from one of the comfortable chairs.

Enjoy TV in your bedroom

For some people the idea of perfect relaxation is to lie in bed and watch the late, late show on TV. The problem often is how to include television attractively in a bedroom decorating plan. A simple solution is an adjustable tension pole that goes from floor to ceiling and can hold a portable TV set. This device uses a minimum of floor space, and it eliminates the need for a TV stand. Slimline TVs are a good choice for the bedroom; they are light and easy to store.

Stacked storage modules fill up a vacant corner efficiently and attractively. Closed, the unit is a display area with an ingenious corner spot for the television set. Open, it reveals roll-out drawers holding mixer, a foldaway bar, areas for record and glassware storage, and snack shelves, all cleverly fitted into the handsome cabinet.

Portable television rolls around the house on a wheeled unit that could double as a serving cart. The television is made less obtrusive by combining it with an attractive grouping of plants and pictures.

Another possibility for reclining television viewers is to build the set into the wall. Remove the framed mirror that hangs over the dresser and build a niche for the television set in its place. Then rehang the mirror, attaching it to the wall with hinges at the side so it can swing away from the TV screen like a door. If another location for a built-in television set is more suitable than over the dresser, it is still possible to conceal the screen when it is not in use. A door that matches those in the room makes an excellent cover-up, and so does a painting on hinges.

Wherever you decide to place your built-in television set in the bedroom, you should bear in mind that your line of vision while reclining is not the same as when you are sitting up. The television set should be placed higher than usual for the most comfortable viewing while in bed. For added convenience, plan to operate your bedroom TV with a remote-control device.

Remember the kitchen

There is no reason why a housewife's hours in her kitchen should be spent in isolation, cut off from the rest of the world. Careful planning, evaluation of kitchen space, and selection of the most suitable size and type of TV can make it possible to keep up with the latest news and special events even while preparing the most elaborate dinner. A kitchen that adjoins a family room can, of course, share its television set, provided that the TV is the type that is on an easy-rolling table or stand. A seldom-used corner of a kitchen counter is an excellent location for one of the smaller, personal-size portable TV sets. Another way to use this type of television set is to perch it at the back of a combination kitchen counter-desk area.

When you plan a new kitchen, or prepare to remodel an old one, consider the advantages and the convenience of building a television set into the wall. A television screen in the 12-to-18-inch-size range will fit well into a floor-to-ceiling unit of cabinets. The screen

One end of this home's living area contains an attractive wall arrangement that is both decorative and functional. It provides a location for the television set; and a few shelves, attached by brackets to metal standards, contain an assortment of items that is visually interesting and whimsical. Interspersed among the shelves are a few colorful pictures. The warmth of the wood-paneled wall is carried over into the cabinets that serve as a base and appear to anchor this unit to the floor. The television set, in a white case that blends into the light color of the wall behind it, is unobtrusive and at the same time well located on top of the base cabinets.

should be readily visible from all parts of the kitchen, especially from the eating area.

If space is at a premium in your kitchen, and you cannot afford the room necessary to put a built-in TV among your cabinets, there are some alternate possibilities. In the eating area of a kitchen that has a hutch or other arrangement of cabinets, use some of the space to incorporate a television set and conceal it behind a pair of matching doors. For a small kitchen eating area where there is no room for cabinets or a built-in TV, make a simple wall arrangement of stained or painted shelves, either to match or contrast with your color scheme. Attach them to the wall with brackets of wood or metal. One of the shelves should easily accommodate your portable television set. Use some of the remaining shelf space for a kitchen library of cookbooks. This is also a good location for a copy of your local telephone directory and your personal telephone book. Other additions might include a calendar and a blackboard. Add one or two small green plants for color and you have created an attractive TV viewing area in your kitchen.

There is no need for a blank television screen to be a distraction in your living room or anywhere else. Here is one way to conceal your TV when it is not in use. The set in this living room is recessed behind four pictures on a sliding panel. The pictures are mounted flush with the panel edges to disguise it even more. When the panel is pushed to the right, the TV screen is ready for viewing; pushed back in place it is a decorative picture group.

The built-in buffet in this family room is a piece of furniture of many surprises. At the far end is a serving cart. Dishes and other entertainment accessories are stored in the center cabinets. The first two doors conceal a television set on casters. For comfortable viewing just pull it out to face the sofa and easy chairs at the other end of the room. This ingenious TV arrangement has another convenience for entertaining: its plastic-laminate top is an additional handy serving table.

In this sunny family room, the built-in television set is an integral part of the decorating plan. Housed in a specially scaled compartment, the TV is concealed when not in use by folding doors covered in laminated plastic. The cabinet, which also holds books and magazines, is an unobtrusive element in the room, painted to blend in with the walls. The hallway where the unit stands was also custom-made, using 4x4-inch floor-to-ceiling posts as dividers to define the area and screen entrances and exits. For TV viewing, the chairs are simply turned around.

Master/Guide

Siamoise

A Victorian seating piece consisting of two chairs (often completely upholstered) joined at the sides but facing in opposite directions. The structure (seen from above) thus formed an S shape. This type of chair was also known as a *tête-à-tête* or a *conversational*. The design is thought to have first developed in France during the 1850s. For information about Victorian furniture, see *Furniture Styles,* Vol. 9, p. 1626.

Side Chair

A term loosely used to distinguish a chair without arms from a chair constructed with side rails intended to function as armrests. Developed during the early Renaissance, the side chair was considered, in terms of ornament and function, as ranking between the stool and the more dignified armchair. Although the derivation of the term is obscure, it would seem that this kind of chair was originally intended to be placed against a wall or to the "side" of a dominant piece of furniture.

Side Table (and Sideboard)

Any of a variety of ornamental tables designed to be set against a wall. During the eighteenth century, side tables were decorated chiefly on the front facade. The side table soon evolved into more complex forms intended to be used as serving and storage pieces. During the late eighteenth century, the side table evolved into the sideboard (or combination chest and table) as we know it in modern furniture.

Siena Marble

A variety of marble found in the area of Tuscany. Siena marble has a light orange hue broken by streaks of black and purple. The term frequently refers to any light-colored marble.

Signed Furniture

A term used to refer to antique or handcrafted furniture that carries the name or initials of the maker. In French furniture, the initials were either burnt or stamped into an inconspicuous portion of the furniture.

Silk

The strong and lustrous filaments derived from the cocoon of the silkworm (the larva of the silk moth), and also a cloth made from them. The techniques used in cultivating the silkworm, harvesting the filaments from the cocoon, and spinning a yarn from the filaments were obtained from China during the Middle Ages. Among the best known of silk cloths are satin and velvet.

Silk Screening

A method of transferring a pattern to fabric, paper, or a similar material by means of a silk

Pop artist Andy Warhol's self portrait. Warhol is one of the leading modern exponents of silk screening.

screen stretched in a frame and used in the manner of a stencil. The area of the silk that is not to print has been treated with a substance that causes it to become nonporous. By means of a brush or roller, ink is passed over the screen and thus transferred through the areas of the silk that have not been treated. For every color in the printed design, a different color screen (in a corresponding pattern) must be used.

Silver and Pewter Holloware

Vessels and dishes made from silver or pewter. The term *holloware* is used in contrast to *flatware,* which refers to knives, forks, and similar utensils. For a discussion of types, qualities, and care, see *Silver and Pewter Holloware,* p. 2883.

Silvering

The application of silver ornament to furniture. Gilded or varnished silver leaf was sometimes used as a less-expensive substitute for gold leaf. The term is also used to refer to the preparation of mirrors by using silver backing to create the reflective surface behind the glass.

Skirt

The flat board that extends beneath a surface such as a tabletop, chair seat, or shelf. Also known as an *apron* or *frieze,* this board is usually embellished with carving or applied decoration. The term is also used to refer to a strip of fabric put along the bottom of a chair or sofa covering in order to hide the furniture legs.

Skylight

A glassed-in opening in a roof. Often a skylight can be opened to permit the entrance of air as well as light. For a discussion of the advantages and installation of this feature, see *Skylights,* p. 2888.

Slant-Front Writing Desk

An eighteenth-century desk that had a drop-lid writing surface (supported on lopers when dropped) set above a series of spacious drawers.

The unit rested on bracket feet. When closed, the drop-lid rested at an angle (or slant) against the back of the desk. Although the design varied, this style of desk was continuously popular in England and America during the eighteenth and nineteenth centuries.

Slat Back

A chair back, introduced in the late seventeenth century, that was formed of horizontal slats joined to the chair-back uprights. Slat-back chairs are found in a wide variety of designs, one of the best known among them being the English and American ladder-back chair which had a tall and narrow back formed of arched slats, and often had a rush seat. For examples, see *Furniture Styles,* Vol. 9, p. 1626.

Slate

A dark brittle stone easily cut into plates suitable for roofing and flooring.

Sleigh Bed

An early-nineteenth-century American bed with a heavy construction (often veneered with mahogany) and thick lines, derived in style from the French Empire couch. The bedstead had a lyre form, high and outwardly curving head- and footboards; it received its name from the fact that its head and foot each suggested the front of a sleigh.

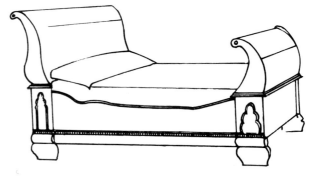

Sliding Glass Door

A glass door that opens by sliding to one side along a permanent axis rather than changing its axis to open forward or backward. For more information, see *Sliding Glass Doors,* p. 2892.

Sling Chair

A modern chair composed of a metal rod frame with a canvas (or leather) seat draped from it. The metal rods are ingeniously bent into a shape that forms two raised angles in the back (thus resembling the uprights of a conventional chair) and two lower angles in the front. The material suspended from these angles thus forms a sloping scoop. The sling chair is also known as the Hardoy chair after the modern designer, Ferrari-Hardoy, who was partly responsible for its development. For a discussion of modern chair design, see *Modern Furniture,* Vol. 12, p. 2208.

Slip (and Slipware)

Clay mixed with water to produce a thick or thin paste used to fix decorations or functional parts to the body of a clay object ready for firing. The term *slipware* is applied to the more extensive use of slip in producing color patterns.

Seventeenth-century example of slipware. The design was added in a contrasting slip, a suspension of clay in water.

Slipcover

A cover of fabric, plastic, or a similar material that can be fitted over an upholstered chair or sofa in order to protect the upholstery or provide added decoration. For more information about these, see *Slipcovers,* p. 2896.

Slipper Chair

A small, very low, armless side chair constructed to provide a comfortable seat for putting on and taking off slippers. The slipper chair, considered an American article of furniture, was introduced in the eighteenth century in the Queen Anne style but became immensely popular during the nineteenth century.

A deeply carved slipper chair of laminated rosewood. Attributed to John Belter. Metropolitan Museum of Art.

Slodtz, Rene Michel (1705-64)

French sculptor, painter, and furniture designer who, together with his brothers Antoine, Sébastien, and Paul, was among the foremost rococo stylists of his day.

Snake Foot

A thick club foot with an elongated head that suggests a snake. The snake foot, like the slipper and claw-and-ball foot, was often found on cabriole legs during the early eighteenth century, particularly on pedestal furniture.

Snap Table

An eighteenth-century side table or serving table, usually with a round top supported by a pedestal rising from three small legs. The top of the table pivoted from a horizontal to a vertical position, thus enabling it to fit more closely against a wall. Also known as a *tip-up table,* the snap table was popular in England and America.

Snuffbox

A small ornate box used during the eighteenth century to carry snuff (powdered tobacco, usually inhaled). Snuffboxes, since they were carried about, were usually made of durable materials such as brass, silver, or ivory.

Enameled and gilded eighteenth-century French snuffbox. Snuffboxes and bottles are favorite collectors' items.

Sofa (and Sofa Bed)

A large seating piece, developed in France during the seventeenth century, that has an upholstered seating platform (for three or more persons), arms on either end, and a continuous back. For more information about traditional and modern sofas, see *Sofas,* p. 2908. The sofa bed is a convertible bed-sofa of modern vintage. The seating platform, unfolding into a sleeping platform, is often useful in small living areas. See *Dual-Purpose Couches,* Vol. 7, p. 1246; and *Dual-Purpose Furniture,* Vol. 7, p. 1250.

Sofa Table

A long, low, and relatively narrow table introduced in the eighteenth century and intended to be placed in front of a sofa. The sofa table often had a small drop-leaf extension on either end. Although the form and decoration varied, some of the finest examples are those designed in the late-eighteenth-century Sheraton style. In a general sense, the sofa table is the forerunner of the modern coffee table.

Soft-Paste Porcelain

Pottery made in imitation of porcelain. Hard-paste, or true porcelain, was imported from China until the secret of its ingredients and proper processing was discovered in the early eighteenth century in Germany. Soft-paste porcelain continued to be produced in abundance, however (particularly in France), until the nineteenth century. Although soft-paste porcelain is less durable than hard-paste, it is capable of more delicate and finished painting.

Sound Control

The reducing or eliminating of loud or excess noise. For a discussion of how to do this in the home, see *Sound Control,* p. 2918.

Souvenir Spoon

An elegant silver or silver-plated spoon decorated with words or pictures that recalled an important event.

Spade Foot

A late-eighteenth-century furniture foot that resembled a blunt tapering rectangle (similar to a spade) whose top was larger than the block-like tapering leg that it terminated. The spade foot was often found on chairs in Hepplewhite or Sheraton styles and it was also favored in American Federal styles.

Spanish Scroll Foot (or Braganza Toe)

An early-eighteenth-century furniture foot of Spanish and Portuguese origin. The Spanish foot splayed outward from a block or a fillet in a vertically ribbed scroll.

Spanish Style

Furniture and decoration distinctly Spanish or Iberian, as influenced by the Moorish occupation. Similar feeling is manifested by Mexican and other Spanish colonial items. For further information, see *Spanish Styles,* p. 2922.

Spice Box (and Spice Chest)

A small, elegant, and ingeniously designed lidded box, often of silver, intended to hold spices. Frequently, such a box rested on tiny decorated feet and the receptacle area was divided into compartments. Spice chests, common articles of furniture during the seventeenth and eighteenth centuries, were small cabinets holding a number of small drawers.

Spider-Leg Table

A light eighteenth-century side table usually with two drop leaves each supported, when raised, by a gate leg. The table received its name from the style of the legs, which were extremely slender and gently turned at the foot. Among the best-known spider-leg tables are those in Sheraton and Chippendale styles.

Spindle (and Split Spindle)

An upright rod (as used, for example, to form the back of a chair) usually turned, blocked, or otherwise elaborated. Spindles, if placed at regular intervals to support a railing, would form a balustrade; thus a spindle can be compared to a baluster. (See also *Stairways,* p. 2928.) Split lengthwise, the resulting half (or split) spindles were sometimes used as applied decorations, especially on seventeenth-century English and American furniture.

Spiral Leg

An eighteenth-century furniture leg that tapered downward in a twisted manner. Of Portuguese origin, the spiral leg was popular on late-eighteenth-century French and English chairs.

Splat

The central portion of a chair back structured in an open style. The splat is variously formed and decorated. Some common varieties are the pierced or solid vase-shaped splat, and lyre, ribbon, and plume-shaped splats.

Splayed Leg (and Splayed Foot)

A furniture leg set at an outward slant. Splayed legs are characteristic, for example, on Windsor chairs and some eighteenth-century chairs that have front legs turned and vertical but back legs splayed. The term is also applied to furniture feet that flare outward.

Splint

A slender strip of hardwood. During the eighteenth century, splints were often woven to form chair seats and backs, as well as serviceable household items such as boxes of various kinds. Splint seats provided an acceptable substitute for the more desirable, but less accessible, rush seats (also known as *flag* seats) characteristic of much provincial furniture.

Split Level

The term used to designate a house whose floors generally are so placed vertically that the level of one is approximately halfway between the positions of the ones above and below it in an adjoining area. For diagrams, descriptions, and discussion of its advantages, see *Split Levels*, p. 2924.

Spode

English pottery produced in Stoke-on-Trent, Staffordshire, from the late eighteenth century to the present. Typical wares are ornately painted, but are of excellent quality.

Spool Furniture

Furniture, such as chairs, tables, and beds, mass produced in America during the nineteenth century. The furniture receives its name from the characteristic beadlike turnings that were used to form uprights and horizontal railings. Although quaint and often constructed from mediocre wood, spool furniture is typically Victorian in its relationship to the Elizabethan and cottage-style revivals of the period.

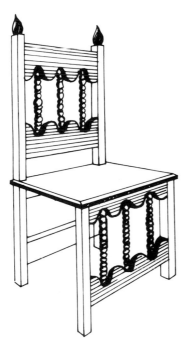

Spoon-Back (and Spoon-Back Chair)

A tall chair back formed by a slight outward curve, the combined back and legs suggesting (from the side) the double curve of the conventional spoon. Borrowed from the Dutch, the style was briefly popular in England during the Queen Anne period. The term spoon-back chair is also applied to an Empire-style chair (also known as a Madame Jumel chair) that had a back and arms formed by a continuous descending arch.

Spoon Rack

A small wooden wall plaque fixed with slotted rails for holding spoons. Spoon racks have been common and simple articles of household furniture since Elizabethan times.

Sprigged Ware

Eighteenth-century English pottery decorated with patterns composed of twigs, leaves, flowers. The motifs were formed in molds and applied to the pottery base by means of slip. This form of ornament was called sprigging.

Staffordshire

The name given to a great variety of kinds and qualities of pottery produced in works centering in the clay-rich county of Staffordshire, England, from the sixteenth century to the present. The range of wares include practical and boldly

Eighteenth-century Staffordshire soup tureen with tortoiseshell salt glaze and applied foliage designs.

Whistler's Peacock Room is covered in costly stamped Spanish leather, which Whistler painted over.

painted plates and mugs, transfer-printed items (both of these largely intended for the nineteenth-century American market), as well as the more refined and expensive varieties of Wedgewood and Spode.

Stained Glass
An art form, most fully developed during the Middle Ages, in which patterns and pictorial scenes are formed by means of pieces of colored glass held together by lead strips. Medieval stained-glass windows are among the greatest works of Western art.

Stairway
In architecture, a stepped structure providing access from one level to another. For a discussion of stairways in decoration, and of how to build certain types, see *Stairways*, p. 2928.

Stamped Leather
Leather, usually prepared in large rectangular shapes, that has been decorated with stamped or raised patterns. The patterns were often painted or gilded. Originating in Spain and Italy, leather work of this variety was often used as wall hangings during the Renaissance.

Kennebunkport "Wedding Cake House," *c*. 1850, is decorated with typical Steamboat Gothic gingerbread.

Standish

An article of desk furniture also known as an inkstand. Common since the seventeenth century, the standish has varied in size, structure, and quality, but it was usually a metal or wooden tray or platform that held an inkpot and another container for blotting sand.

Star Molding

A narrow molding decorated with continuous raised stars. The star motif has long been a popular form of decoration on furniture.

Steamboat Gothic

The name given to nineteenth-century wooden ornamentation composed of elaborately turned finials, railings, and open paneling used on cabinets, porches, and similar structures. Also known as "gingerbread," this type of ornament is thought to have been borrowed from the typical decoration of the Mississippi steamboats.

Steeple Clock

A nineteenth-century wooden mantle clock originating in New England and designed in the shape of a steeple flanked by narrow spires in a Gothic style. The clock face was placed near the apex of the triangular molding that formed the gabled "roof" between the spires. The lower rectangular platform was a small closed-door cabinet housing the clock works.

Stencil

A sheet of paper or metal into which patterns have been cut. The pattern is transferred to a piece of furniture or wall surface by brushing paint over the sheet. During the nineteenth century, stencil work was used to decorate walls and to embellish inexpensive furniture.

Stepped Curve

A curved shape broken by a right angle, or "step." During the eighteenth century, stepped curves were sometimes employed on the top moldings of the crests of chair backs.

Sterling

The term, indicative of quality, applied to silverware that is composed of over 90 percent pure silver, or 925 parts silver and 75 parts copper. For a discussion of silver quality, see *Hallmarks,* Vol. 10, p. 1775.

Stickley, Gustav (1857-1942)

American furniture designer responsible for the early-twentieth-century revival of furniture in the style of the English Arts and Crafts movement and the Spanish colonial tradition. Such wooden furniture was simple, rugged, and unadorned. Mass produced, it was widely distributed and enjoyed considerable popularity during the first decades of the century.

Stiegel, Heinrich Wilhelm (1729-85)

American (of German birth) glass designer and manufacturer who developed a glassworks in Manheim, Pennsylvania. By employing skilled European labor, Stiegel was able to imitate the fine quality of English flint glass. Although the

An example of the fine craftsmanship found in products of the Steigel glassworks. Metropolitan Museum of Art.

Stiegel works went into bankruptcy in 1774, it has had considerable influence upon the evolution of American glassmaking.

Stipple Engraving

In engraving, a technique of producing tonal value by filling areas with dots or tiny lines. The term *stippling* refers to any shaded area produced by creating tone through discrete dots rather than solid color.

Stoneware

A very heavy, hard, and nonporous form of pottery related to porcelain. Although known in China at an early date, stoneware was first developed in Europe in Germany during the sixteenth century. Because of its similarity, stoneware is sometimes used to imitate porcelain.

Stool

A seating piece with neither arms nor back. A very ancient article of furniture (known in Egypt as early as 3000 B.C.), the stool is highly versatile. It may have three or four legs, a round, square, or polygonal seat, and it may serve for seating, storage (with a drawer beneath the seat), or as a footrest.

Storage

A place for storing items of various kinds. For ideas on where to locate storage, how to build many forms of it, and how to use it in decorating schemes, see *Storage and Storage Walls,* p. 2938.

Stretcher (or Underbrace)

A (usually) horizontal rail or member connecting and strengthening the legs of tables, chairs, sofas, stools, and similar pieces.

Stringing (and Strings)

Inlaid veneer in a thin band. These bands were placed near and along the edges of veneered furniture surfaces, thus forming a frame (usually of a strongly contrasting color). Stringing was a popular mode of decoration in eighteenth-

and early-nineteenth-century furniture. The term *strings* is sometimes applied to the tiny square pieces of veneer used to compose the band.

Nineteenth-century satinwood English corner cabinet is decorated with delicate veneer stringing.

Striped Glass

A late-nineteenth-century American art glass characterized by wavy bands of color against a differently colored ground. The color is produced by first embedding the glass with canes (filaments) of colored glass. The technique and effect produced is derived from traditional Venetian glassmaking.

Stucco

A form of durable plaster or cement used to cover inside or outside walls. The surface of the stucco is often impressed with a texture as it is applied and sometimes the plaster composition includes glass fragments or similar material to enhance the brilliance of the effect.

Intricate friezes and swirling designs in stucco decorate this sixteenth-century Venetian ceiling.

Studio Apartment

A small city apartment usually composed of one room. For a discussion of how to furnish and decorate such apartments, see *Studio Apartments,* p. 2978.

Studio Couch

An upholstered couch, usually without back or arms, that can be converted into a bed in any of various fashions.

Study Area

A small area equipped with the furniture and accessories necessary for and conducive to study. For a discussion of how to decorate and prepare these areas, see *Study Areas,* p. 2986.

Stump Foot Furniture Leg

A furniture leg that ends at the bottom without terminating in a distinctive change in the shape of the leg. In traditional furniture, the back legs of chairs are often treated in a stump-foot manner, even though the front legs may terminate in a styled foot.

Sugar Pine

A soft wood native to the western regions of the United States. It has a light reddish-brown color and a fine, muted, and consistent grain. Sugar pine is used in wall paneling and for the interior structure of furniture.

Sunburst

A risen-sun motif, variously styled, used in all the decorative arts. The motif, symbolic of majesty and power, is most commonly depicted as an orb from which numerous and distinct rays radiate. It is more specifically associated with the ornamental styles of Louis XIV, *Le Roi Soleil,* the Sun King.

Sunfast

In textiles, a term used to refer to dyed goods that are able to resist fading when exposed to sunlight.

Sun Filter

A roof or screen to provide partial shade over an otherwise exposed area around the home. A discussion of the decorating merits and practical advantages, as well as how to build them, will be found under *Sun Filters,* p. 2992.

Sun Porch

A screened or (frequently) glass-enclosed porch or outside room of a house that has a sunny exposure. For a discussion of their advantages, see *Sun Porches,* p. 2996.

Surrealism

An uniquely important twentieth-century art movement that emphasized the role of the subconscious mind. Surrealistic painting and sculpture are often of a fantastic nature, presenting real objects in an unreal setting. The roots of the movement can be traced to the medieval painter Hieronymus Bosch and others. Modern masters of this idiom include Salvador Dali, Paul Klee, and Giorgio di Chirico.

The fusion of reality and irrationality that typifies Surrealism is exemplified in this work by Salvador Dali.

Swag

Cloth gathered and draped in a single curve or a series of similar curves. For examples, see *Windows and Window Treatments,* Vol. 17 and Vol. 18. The term is also used to refer to the same effect in a carved motif in furniture.

Swan, Abraham

An eighteenth-century English furniture designer whose book, *The British Architect, or The Builder's Treasury of Staircases,* strongly influenced English and American Georgian architecture and furnishings.

Swan-Neck (and Swan-Neck Pediment)

A term broadly applied to any slightly S-curved member. The swan-neck, a popular style of cabinet pediment during the eighteenth century,

was a broken pediment flanked by facing curved moldings with the open space between occupied by a decorative finial. Other common pediment styles are the arched and triangular pediments.

Swansea

Porcelain produced during the eighteenth and nineteenth centuries in Swansea, Wales. Although typical wares were often an imitation of Staffordshire products, Swansea soft-paste porcelain, in early-nineteenth-century neoclassic styles, was distinctive and original.

Swedish Modern

A term used to refer to contemporary furniture styles originating in Sweden, particularly during the 1920s and 1930s; these styles were strongly influenced by the furniture developed in the German Bauhaus experiments. The furniture was functional, strongly linear, and emphasized light unadorned woods. Among the most eminent of Swedish designers were Alvar Aalto and Bruno Mathsson. For more information, see *Modern Furniture,* Vol. 12, p. 2208.

Swell Front

A term used to refer to furniture with a front facade in the shape of a convex curve. Similar terms are bombé, bow, and serpentine. *Bombé* is more often used with reference to French furniture, *serpentine* to English.

Swimming Pool

For home use, a modest-sized enclosure filled with water to provide a place for swimming. See *Swimming Pools,* p.3002, for information about types, costs, installation, and decorative aspects of home swimming pools.

Sycamore

A light-colored hardwood popular particularly for veneers and inlays. When treated chemically, the wood turns a greenish color that was favored during the eighteenth century for marquetry; in this condition it is known as *harewood.*

Symmetrical

A term used to refer to any arrangement that has two equal halves, the one half a reverse of the other. For a discussion of symmetrical furniture placement, see *Furniture Arrangement,* Vol. 9, p. 1552. Symmetry is generally regarded as an attribute of classic design.

Tabernacle Mirror

A late-eighteenth- and early-nineteenth-century American mirror intended to be hung from a wall. Styled in the neoclassic manner, the mirror frame was formed by gilded flanking columns that supported a cornice. Tiny balls or acorns were attached in a row under the cornice. The upper portion of the unit contained a painting, usually of a historical, and patriotic, event.

Tabernacle mirrors were popular in America between 1790 and 1820. Photo courtesy of Metropolitan Museum of Art.

Table

A traditional basic article of furniture composed of a flat surface on legs or on a pedestal. The table has developed in a great variety of forms and decorative treatments, and its versatility has permitted it to be adapted to many different functions. For a discussion, see *Tables,* p. 3012.

Table Setting and Linen

The items placed upon a table used as a dining surface. For a discussion of decorative values and appropriateness of styles and arrangements, see *Table Settings and Linens,* p. 3026.

Tabouret

A small richly upholstered or carved stool used as a side chair during the seventeenth and early eighteenth centuries. The term is also applied to a small storage unit with shelves and drawers that may have evolved from the stool.

Taffeta

A tightly woven fabric with a lustrous surface and a graceful draping quality, woven from any of several different yarns. Taffeta is often used for bedspreads, draperies, and clothing.

Tallboy

A large eighteenth-century English chest of drawers composed of a chest-on-chest (distinct upper and lower units) or a chest set upon a table (which may itself have contained drawers). The tallboy was thus a relative of the more popular highboy and both are the forerunners of the modern bureau.

Tall-Case Clock

A large traditional floor clock in the shape of a pillar. The clock works are housed in the shaft and the clock face appears in the capital. This clock is also known as a gradfather's clock, and a smaller version of it is known as a grandmother's clock.

Talon-and-Ball Foot

An alternate name for the popular eighteenth-century claw-and-ball foot. Often found on cabriole legs, the talon-and-ball foot was an Oriental motif introduced into Europe by the Dutch in the seventeenth century.

Tambour

A sliding panel composed of strips of wood glued to a cloth backing, usually canvas, in order to make the panel flexible enough to slide in an arc, as, for example, to cover the writing area of a roll-top desk. This construction was introduced during the eighteenth century and was often used on cabinets and desks in the Hepplewhite and Sheraton styles.

Tankard

Traditionally, a large mug with a hinged cover, used for drinking beer. Tankards were made from silver, pewter, horn, and sometimes ceramics.

Tatami

A thin straw mat of Japanese origin popularly used as a floor or wall covering.

Teak

A hard, durable, light-brown wood native to the East Indies. Teak has strong black markings and has become particularly popular in modern wood furniture.

Television

A popular form of entertainment in the home. The article *Television,* p. 3048, gives an exposition of the places and ways to locate your set from the viewpoint of the best decorating.